POWER
Pressure
Cooking

Eric Theiss

Published by Cheer Master, Ltd and Tristar Products, Inc.

Printed in China.

**Publisher's Cataloging-in-Publication
(Provided by Quality Books, Inc.)**

Theiss, Eric, author.
    Power pressure cooking with Eric Theiss.
    pages cm
    Includes index.

    1. Pressure cooking. 2. Cooking, American.
    3. Cookbooks.   I. Title.

TX840.P7T44 2015   641.5'87
                        QBI15-600163

Acknowledgements

I needed all hands on deck to write this cookbook! I could not have done it without my "right-hand woman," my wife Jesse, who worked endless hours on writing, editing, testing and tasting recipes. My two sons, Cameron and Max, served as unbiased taste testers of the recipes I wrote and tested, happily giving me the "thumbs up" or "thumbs down" using the philosophy that brutal honesty is the best policy. To my mom, Arlene, thank you for taking me to the library to check out my first cookbook as a little boy. You always knew in what direction I was headed before I did.

To Meredith Laurence, not just my business partner but also my friend, thank you for putting up with me during this project and for always knowing what I mean and fixing what I say.

I want to call out the hard work of all of the other key people who helped me bring this book to fruition: Kris "Chez" Amerine for getting me through writer's block, my food stylists extraordinaire Lynn Willis, Bonne Di Tomo and Lisa Ventura, photographer Jessica Walker, as well as Joseph McAllister, Clive Pyne for the excellent book indexing services, Laurie Leiker and my friend and book designer, Janis Boehm. A special thanks to Jessica Moyer and Peter Asmus for the generous use of their kitchen during the photo shoot for this cookbook.

Table of Contents

About the Author

Eric Theiss's culinary savoir-faire started in northern New Jersey as a child when his Italian mother, on a hunch, borrowed from the public library his first cookbook at age 6. His mother was right, and Eric began a life of culinary work. As a young adult, he continued to fuel his passion for food and fine dining. During his early twenties, his love of food and wine manifested itself in working long nights in NJ restaurants, including his favorite kitchen of all at The Culinary Renaissance, where acclaimed chef Frank Falcinelli[1] exposed Eric to a level of culinary passion that inspired Eric to strive. In 1997 he took a leap of faith and opened his own fine dining restaurant and bar called Meritage in West Chester, PA–one that enjoyed rave reviews from some prominent Philadelphia food critics. Here, his dream of owning and operating a fine dining establishment was fully realized.

A few years later, utilizing his inventive and creative flair, Eric moved on to the culinary broadcast world, working in product development for not only QVC's proprietary kitchenware lines but also for celebrity lines (Paula Deen, Emeril, Rocco DiSpirito, Rachael Ray) as well as his own personal line of cool kitchen tools and cookware, Walah!. Eric has been a popular regular TV Chef presenter for over 10 years on QVC's live shows for his own brands as well as a variety of well-known national kitchen brands. Beyond that, Eric owns and operates a company that brokers into QVC many new and innovative products. His most recent business venture, a successful new publishing company (also named Walah!), publishes cookbooks and pamphlets and distributes them nationwide.

Paramount to his career thus far, Eric currently hosts, among others, the incredibly successful, award-winning long-form infomercial featuring the Power Pressure Cooker XL, which has sold over a million units and has achieved a TOP 5 status. Eric wrote this cookbook to complement the pressure cooker infomercial, and it answers customers' call for delicious, easy recipes.

Eric currently resides near the live studios at QVC in PA along with his wife Jessica and his two sons, Cameron and Maxwell.

[1] Owner of NY Restaurants Frankies 457, Frankies Sputino, Prime Meats and Café Pedlar.

Pressure Cooker Q & A

Q: Are pressure cookers safe?

A: The short answer is yes! The new pressure cookers, especially the electric pressure cookers, are extremely safe. They have several safety features built in to avoid clogging and over heating. In most cases the new electric pressure cookers will turn off the heat supply if temperatures get too high. Thanks to the cycling of heat in electric pressure cookers, there is no need for the constant, frightening screeching of the old fashioned "jiggle valves" found on older manual pressure cookers. The modern day electric pressure cookers have many built in safety features that prevent pressure build up if the lid is not closed properly and they also prevent the lid from opening until all pressure has been released.

Q: How long have pressure cookers been in existence.

A:

- While pressure cookers were first invented in the 1600's, they didn't become a common household item until the beginning of the 20th Century.

- Pressure cookers were originally called "steam digesters" when invented by physicist Denis Papin in London.

- The first pressure cookers sold commercially were made of tinned cast iron. Now the best pressure cookers are made of stainless steel.

- The first pressure cooker cookbook was published in Spain in 1924 and included 360 recipes specifically for the cooker.

Q: Do pressure cookers use more energy?

A: No, this is thanks to the efficiency of pressure cooking. Using only a small amount of energy to maintain pressure is the key. Cooking time is faster—often 1/3 to ½ the amount of traditional cooking times—and your kitchen remains much cooler.

Q. Are pressure cookers hard to cook in?

A: NO! In fact, they are very easy to cook in. In most cases, it is just a matter of putting at least a cup of liquid and your food into the cooker, locking the lid and choosing a cook time. What's nice about cooking in a modern electric pressure cooker is that you don't need to stand around and tend to the food as it cooks. You literally walk away and let it do its job!

Q: Are pressure cookers hard to clean?

A: No, for a few reasons. Most electric pressure cookers are nonstick. The inner pot is easily removed and because you are cooking under super heat and steam, you rarely have a baked-on mess. Most pressure cooker meals are cooked in one pot all at once so there are fewer pans to clean. Splatter is eliminated thanks to the lid, which is locked on during cooking.

Q: Why is pressure cooking so much faster than traditional cooking?

A: The answer can be long and boring, but it's actually very simple. Pressure cooking raises the temperature of the liquid from a 212° F boiling point up to approximately 240° F. It may not sound like much, but being able to cook hotter enables faster cooking, and in some cases up to 70% faster.

Q: If cooking in a pressure cooker is hotter than traditional cooking does that mean all of the nutrients are destroyed?

A: No, pressure cooking nutrition has been studied for a long time, and in many cases pressure cooking will retain more nutrients than traditional methods. Cooking foods for less time at higher temperatures is easier on nutrients, vitamins and minerals than the stovetop or the oven is. Boiling vegetables, for example, causes the nutrients to leach out into the water and escape through steam vapor. Then we dump the water with the nutrients down the drain. Pressure cookers trap the steam and the nutrients inside the pot. One 2007 study published in the *Journal of Food and Science* showed that broccoli maintained 92% of its Vitamin C when pressure cooked as opposed to the 78% that was maintained through boiling the broccoli. There have also been studies to show that pressure cooking can make many hard-to-digest foods easier to digest.

Q: Is pressure cooking healthy?

A: In many cases no fats or oils are needed to create great tasting food, which creates leaner, lighter results. Also, because pressure cooking is so fast and easy, it makes it less likely that you will need to order unhealthy take out or fast food after a long day or when you are in a pinch for time.

Q: Is pressure cooking environmentally friendly?

A: More than ever before, people seek healthy alternatives and whole foods. Pressure cookers make it easy to cook whole foods and you retain a higher percentage of the nutrients when pressure cooking. Also, because it takes less time to cook under pressure, we are using less power resources to cook. Saving energy is good for the environment and for your bills.

Q: What is a gasket and why is it an important part of the pressure cooker?

A: The lid of the pressure cooker is lined with a flexible (rubber or silicone) ring that goes around the entire circumference of the lid and allows the lid to create an airtight seal. It is important to make sure you clean and dry the gasket after each use, and they are easy to take in and out of the lid. Follow your instruction manual so that you do this properly. Your gasket should last many years, but if it ever appears dried out, cracked or stiffened, you should replace it with a new one. Most manufacturers will recommend replacing your gasket annually if you pressure cook regularly.

Q: What do they mean by "quick release" and "natural release" when releasing the pressure in my pressure cooker?

A: Most pressure cookers come equipped with a pressure regulator that is built into the lid. These valves release excess pressure in the event of a malfunction. Every pressure cooker recipe ends with either a "quick release" which is when you manually open the pressure valve and let the steam out quickly or "natural release," which is when you simply turn off the cooker and let the steam escape gradually and naturally without opening the valve manually. Just follow the recipe's instructions to know which is best for which recipe.

Q: What makes pressure-cooked food so tasty?

A: Pressure cookers are renowned for creating super tasty meals in less time. That's because super heated steam pounds the food with pressure while the flavors and ingredients cannot escape the unit. Because all of the goodness stays inside the cooker, the food comes out with intense flavor. Beyond that, cuts of meat that contain the most flavor tend to be the ones that are usually tougher to make tender through cooking. The pressure cooker cooks at higher temperatures, so that breaks down the meat fast, making it juicy and fall-apart tender.

Q: Can I brown or "sear" my food in a pressure cooker?

A: As with the Power Pressure Cooker XL, most electric pressure cookers have a browning or searing mode. In the PPCXL, you simply turn the unit on and push any one of the preset cooking buttons to put the unit into browning mode. Once the food and liquid is added and the lid is locked, the unit switches to pressure cooking mode. Other brands of pressure cookers may have buttons labeled "browning" or "searing" mode.

Q: Can I steam in the pressure cooker?

A: YES! Many electric pressure cookers come with a steaming rack, and all you have to do is pour water into the pot and using the steaming rack, place the ramekins, ceramic dish, or even metal baker onto the rack.

Q: Can I put frozen foods into my pressure cooker?

A: Yes. Just remember to add an extra 10 minutes for frozen meats.

Q: How long will it take the pressure cooker to come to pressure and start cooking?

A: This can take anywhere from a few minutes to up to 17 minutes, depending on the ingredients and the amount of liquid in the cooker and the temperature of the ingredients. For instance, frozen raw wings will take longer to pressurize than the same amount of raw thawed wings, etc.

Q: If there is steam coming out of my lid, is that normal?

A: No. If there is steam coming out of the sides of your pressure cooker and the pressure valve is in the closed position, then the lid has not sealed correctly. This sometimes happens when the unit is new. Check that your gasket ring is in place. Also try pushing down on the lid to create the tight seal and stop the steam from escaping. Check your instruction manual for further troubleshooting ideas. Aside from some slight hissing and spitting of steam as the unit comes to pressure, the only steam that should escape the cooker is when the cooking is finished and the steam is releasing from the pressure release valve.

The Finishing Touch

Eric's Recipe Tips for Pressure Cooking

No matter what pressure cooker you're using, you need to always use AT LEAST one cup of liquid to cook your food. It doesn't really matter what that liquid is (water, broth, wine, etc), depending on the recipe. Because no liquid escapes the cooker in the form of steam, there is no "reduction" or evaporation. This is a good thing, because it keeps much of the flavor and nutrients intact. I like to use the least amount of liquid necessary for almost all recipes except for soups and stocks because it yields a more concentrated result. When I want a thicker result for my gravy, sauce or stew, there are many different ways to achieve that. Here are some of the ways I do this:

ROUX—This is the most classic way to thicken sauces, soups, stews, etc. A roux is an equal mixture of wheat flour and fat (traditionally butter). The butter is melted in a small pot and then the flour is added. The mixture is stirred until the flour is well incorporated and the desired color has been achieved, about 2-3 minutes usually. The end result is a thickening agent to be added to your sauce, gravy or stew. If you use 1 oz. (2 tbsp.) of flour and 1 oz. (2 tbsp.) of butter, for instance, you could add that to a volume 8 times larger (in this case, 1 cup of your gravy or sauce) and it would be correctly proportioned as a thickening agent.

SLURRY—Sometimes a slurry is preferable because you use ½ the amount of cornstarch to thicken that you would of flour. Also, it is gluten free and usually lump free. To make a "slurry," mix one tablespoon of cornstarch with a ½ cup of cold water. Whisk until blended well and thickened. Add it to your sauce or gravy in the pressure cooker and, using the browning feature, bring it to a boil for just a few seconds, then hit the cxl/warm button to reduce the heat.

INSTANT POTATO FLAKES—I don't remember how I found out about his trick, but I feel it is the easiest of all thickening methods. Simply add a ¼ cup of instant potato flakes to your sauce, gravy or stew and stir. After a couple of minutes, if you want an even thicker result, simply sprinkle in more flakes until desired thickness is achieved. This does not interfere with the flavor of your meal.

SIMMERING—By simply utilizing the browning mode after you remove the lid from the pressure cooker, you can reduce your sauce or gravy using evaporation. If using the Power Pressure Cooker XL, remember that pushing any of the preset buttons will put you into browning mode as long as the lid is off.

BUTTER—In a lot of cases, I like to add a tablespoon or two of butter (depending on the volume of the sauce/gravy) at the end of the cooking process. This adds a really nice shimmer and "mouth feel" to the sauce or gravy you've cooked.

TOMATO PASTE—A staple that I use a lot in my dishes is tomato paste. If tomato is a flavor profile that you are adding to your dish, tomato paste is a great way to do that and it adds a thickness and richness to the final result. The paste will really shine through if you choose to reduce the sauce by simmering.

DRIED HERBS—Just as in traditional cooking, you can use dried herbs during the cooking process but should not use them to "finish" the dish. In many cases, in the pressure cooker recipes you will use a lesser amount of dried herbs because no flavor is lost and, in fact, flavors will be intensified during the pressure cooking process.

FRESH HERBS—Wherever possible, I always recommend finishing the dishes you cook with chopped fresh herbs. This adds brightness and an extra layer of flavor at the end. Most of the time, fresh herbs won't stand up to pressure cooking (or any lengthy cooking for that matter). An exception to this would be what is referred to as a "bouquet garni," which is when you bundle fresh herbs, tie them together with twine and add it to the pot before cooking. An example of a typical bouquet would consist of parsley, basil, rosemary, bay leaf and thyme. This bouquet is removed prior to serving the food. Experiment with other herbs as you wish for stocks, soups and stews.

Converting Recipes

Some folks hesitate to use their pressure cookers because they have their favorite, "go-to" recipes that are written for traditional cooking methods or for slow cookers. Once you get used to pressure cooking, however, you find that it is truly an easy task to convert the recipes for pressure cooking. Here are a few tips on how to do that:

- When converting recipes from traditional recipes, as a general rule you have at least one cup of liquid in the cooker. (Every pressure cooker has a different minimum amount of liquid you need to add. Check your instruction manual.) As a general rule, you can reduce the amount of liquid called for in a traditional recipe by about 20%, as long as you do not go lower than that minimum required by the pressure cooker.

- When converting from a regular recipe to a pressure cooker recipe, cut the time down to one-third of the original time, as a general rule.

- **I have included a conversion chart in this cookbook for your convenience**, but as a general rule, follow these guidelines. If you're trying to convert a recipe from a smaller pressure cooker to a larger one multiply the ingredients by the difference in the size of the pressure cooker. So if for example your pressure cooker calls for 1 cup of carrots in the 4 quart cooker, you would increase that my 30% and use ⅓ cups of carrots in the 6 quart cooker. Conversely, if your recipe is written for an 8 quart pressure cooker, and you are using a 6 quart cooker, you would divide the ingredients by 25%. In this case you would use ¾ cup of carrots if the 8 quart called for 1 cup of carrots. **Important reminder:** If you are left with less than a cup of liquid, though, increase the liquid to one cup.

- One thing to keep in mind too is that a lot of the recipes will work in more than one size cooker without even changing the proportions, as long as you aren't filling the cooker past its MAX FILL line. This works the other way too. If you have a recipe for a 6 quart, you can use a larger pressure cooker and simply not fill it up.

- For converting stews from slow cooker recipes, remember to brown your meat first in the pressure cooker using the browning mode. Also, since pressure cookers use steam generated in the pot, make sure you don't fill the pressure cooker pot more than 2/3 full of food, or half full of liquids, to make sure you have room for steam to generate.

- If you are cooking a recipe in which the liquid called for is proportionate to the solid ingredients, never cook less than what 1 cup of liquid makes.

Conversion Chart

Measurements for 6qt pressure cooker	4qt	8qt	10qt
Teaspoons			
1/2	1/4	3/4	1
3/4	1/2	1	1 1/4
1	3/4	1 1/4	1 3/4
1 1/4	3/4	1 3/4	2
1 1/2	1	2	2 1/2
Tablespoons			
1	3/4	1 1/4	1 3/4
2	1 1/4	2 3/4	3 1/4
3	2	4	5
4	2 3/4	5 1/4	6 3/4
Cups			
1/4	1/4	1/3	1/2
1/2	1/3	2/3	3/4
3/4	1/2	1	1 1/4
1	2/3	1 1/3	1 2/3
1 1/4	3/4	1 2/3	2
1 1/2	1	2	2 1/2
1 3/4	1 1/4	2 1/3	3
2	1 1/3	2 2/3	3 1/3
2 1/4	1 1/2	3	3 3/4
2 1/2	1 2/3	3 1/3	4 1/4
2 3/4	1 3/4	3 2/3	4 1/2
3	2	4	5
3 1/4	2 1/4	4 1/3	5 1/2
3 1/2	2 1/3	4 2/3	5 3/4
3 3/4	2 1/2	5	6 1/4
4	2 2/3	5 1/3	6 2/3
4 1/4	2 3/4	5 2/3	7
4 1/2	3	6	7 1/2
4 3/4	3 1/4	6 1/3	8
5	3 1/3	6 2/3	8 1/3
5 1/4	3 1/2	7	8 3/4
5 1/2	3 2/3	7 1/3	9 1/4
5 3/4	3 3/4	7 2/3	9 1/2

Measurements for 6qt pressure cooker	4qt	8qt	10qt
Pounds			
1	2/3	1 1/3	1 2/3
1 1/2	1	2	2 1/2
2	1 1/3	2 2/3	3 1/3
2 1/2	1 2/3	3 1/3	4 1/4
3	2	4	5
3 1/2	2 1/3	4 2/3	5 3/4
4	2 2/3	5 1/3	6 2/3
4 1/2	3	6	7 1/2
5	3 1/3	6 2/3	8 1/3
Ounces			
1	1/2	1 1/2	2
2	1	2 1/2	3
3	2	4	5
4	3	5	7
5	3	7	8
6	4	8	10
7	5	9	12
8	5	11	13
9	6	12	15
10	7	13	17
11	7	15	18
12	8	16	20
13	9	17	22
14	9	19	23
15	10	20	25
16	11	21	27

Equivalent Chart

The charts below use standard U.S. measures following U.S. Government guideline. The charts offer equivalents for United States, metric, and Imperial (U.K.) measures. All conversions are approximate and most have been rounded up or down to the nearest whole number.[1]

Examples below:
1 teaspoon = 4.929 milliliters - rounded up to 5 milliliters
1 ounce = 28.349 grams - rounded down to 28 grams

Dry/Weight Measurements

		Ounces
1/16 teaspoon	a dash	
1/8 teaspoon or less	a pinch or 6 drops	
1/4 teaspoon	15 drops	
1/2 teaspoon	30 drops	
1 teaspoon	1/3 tablespoon	1/6 ounce
3 teaspoons	1 tablespoon	1/2 ounce
1 tablespoon	3 teaspoons	1/2 ounce
2 tablespoons	1/8 cup	1 ounce
4 tablespoons	1/4 cup	2 ounces
5 tablespoons plus 1 teaspoon	1/3 cup	2.6 ounces
8 tablespoons	1/2 cup	4 ounces
10 tablespoons plus 2 teaspoons	2/3 cup	5.2 ounces
12 tablespoons	3/4 cup	6 ounces
16 tablespoons	1 cup	8 ounces
32 tablespoons	2 cups	16 ounces
64 tablespoons	4 cups or 1 quart	32 ounces

Liquid or Volume Measurements

	Pint	Quart	Gallon	U.S. Fluid Ounce	U.S. Tablespoon
jigger or measure	-	-	-	1.5	3
1 cup	1/2	-	-	8	16
2 cups	1	-	-	16	32
4 cups	2	1	1/4	32	64

[1] http://whatscookingamerica.net/Q-A/equiv.htm

13

Pressure Cooking Time Chart

Vegetables	Liquid/Cups	Approximate Minutes
Asparagus, thin whole	1	1-2
Beans, fava	1	4
Beans, green	1	2-3
Beans, lima	1	2
Beets, medium	1	10
Broccoli, pieces	1	2
Brussel sprouts, whole	1	4
Carrots, 1-inch pieces	1	4
Corn, on-the-cob	1	3
Pearl Onions, whole	1	2
Potatoes, 1 1/2" chunks	1	6
Potatoes, whole, medium	1	10-11
Squash, acorn, halved	1	7
Squash, summer, zucchini	1	4

Meats	Liquid/Cups	Approximate Minutes
Beef/Veal, roast or brisket	3-4	35-40
Beef Meatloaf, 2 lbs	1	10-15
Beef, Corned	4	50-60
Pork, roast	1	40-45
Pork, ribs, 2 lbs.	3	20
Leg of Lamb	2-4	35-40
Chicken, whole, 2-3 lbs.	3-4	20
Chicken, pieces, 2-3 lbs.	3-4	15-20
Cornish Hens, two	1	15
Meat/Poultry Soup/Stock	4-6	15-20

Seafood/Fish	Liquid/Cups	Approximate Minutes
Clams	1	2-3
Lobster, 1 1/2 - 2 lbs.	1	2-3
Shrimp	1	1-2
Fish, Soup or Stock	1-4	5-6

NOTE: All pressure cooking modes require the addition of liquid in some form (water, stock, etc.). Unless you are familiar with the pressure cooking process, follow recipes carefully for liquid addition suggestions. Never fill inner pot above MAX line. Always use Pressure Valve to lower pressure quickly.

Word on the Street

What some of my customers are saying...

"My mom used a pressure cooker all the time, but I was always scared of it because of the noise it made. Having tried the new Pressure Cooker XL, I'll never be afraid of it any more. I use it all the time!" Amber R., Cuernavaca, TX

"I use my mom's old pressure cooker at least once a week, so I never had a problem with it. When I went to a friend's who was using the Pressure Cooker XL, I thought it wasn't working because it made no noise. And the food it cooked was awesome!" Julie H., Gardiner, NY

"I've never used a pressure cooker before, but boy, was I surprised when I got the Pressure Cooker XL – I've never seen food cooked so quickly and so well. The meat literally falls off the bone." Kitt C., St. Petersburgh, FL

"I love making chicken noodle soup in the Pressure Cooker XL. All I have to do is put the chicken in, pour in the broth and let it do the cooking. Once the chicken is done, in about 25 minutes, I just add the noodles and it's better than anything I've ever had before, even at a restaurant!" Anne F., Victoria, TX

"I have a big family, so I was skeptical about using a pressure cooker to make pot roast for everyone. I really was shocked when I was able to fill up the Pressure Cooker XL with everything in one pot, set it and when it was done, not only was there enough for everyone, but the meat literally fell apart. Definitely now my go-to, big meal appliance." Jennifer C., Livonia, MI

"I've never used a pressure cooker – just never thought about it. I'm single and always thought you needed to have more people to make a pressure cooker made sense. Boy, was I wrong. I've been cooking a week's worth of meals on Sundays using the pressure cooker, freezing them and now, I'm eating better and saving money while I'm at it!" Rebecca D., Rapid City, SD

"My crock pot was always my go-to kitchen appliance because I could get it set up before I left for work and then just let it cook throughout the day. I won't be doing that much any more, though, because now, it takes less time to use the pressure cooker than it does to set things up before I go to work and then take everything out when I get home. I just come home, put everything in the pressure cooker and within 30 minutes or less, dinner is served!" Michelle O., Wausau, WI

"I started using the recipes that came with the pressure cooker but then started experimenting and now, my friends come over once a week to see what I've come up with in my cooker! Last week, we even made apple pie; there were definitely no left overs." Carol B., Grand Rapids, MI

Soups and Chilies

Soups and Stews are a natural fit for pressure cookers. Using your pressure cooker will not only save you time but also will enhance the flavors. I like to simmer the soups in the pressure cooker once they are done in order to concentrate the flavors even further. After releasing the pressure, take the lid off and in the Power Pressure Cooker simply touch the SOUP/STEW button while you set the table or get your salad ready. In any other type of pressure cooker use your brown/sauté button or the low setting on your stovetop.

For soups, stews and sauces, one of my favorite tips is to add about a ¼ cup of potato flakes at the very end. This will make your stew a bit thicker, which is the way I like it. Of course you could make a roux or a corn starch slurry, which works just as well. You just can't beat the potato flakes for ease of use!

The building blocks of great flavor in a pressure cooker will often start with some type of "stock" or broth, easily produced from scratch in a pressure cooker. You get to use your own ingredients and monitor the salt content, which is often a problem in the store bought stocks. I made sure to include some fast and delicious broths that will help you not only in this section but also in most of the sections in this book. Stocks and broths are easy to freeze and you will definitely save money by making these at home.

**Yields 2 - 3
Quarts**

Making your own broths is a must in the pressure cooker. You get to take advantage of all of the flavors in the bones, yet it doesn't take all day long as it would have on the stovetop in my restaurant. It's very easy to make. Once you start making your own and freezing it, you likely will never buy it in a can again.

Chicken Broth

Ingredients

4 lbs. chicken meat and bones

2 medium onions, chopped

3 tbsp. olive oil

3 carrots, chopped

3 stalks of celery, chopped

5 cloves of garlic

2 tbsp. whole black peppercorns

2 tsp. whole coriander seed

1 tbsp. kosher salt

3 bay leaves

½ bunch of fresh thyme

1 tbsp. tomato paste

1 cup white wine

3 quarts cold water

Directions

1.   Add oil to pot and push CHICKEN/MEAT button then the time adjustment button to reach 40 minutes (high pressure 40 min).

2.   Season chicken and bones generously with salt and pepper, then, when the oil is hot, sear to a deep brown. Remove and set aside.

3.   Add onions, carrot, celery, garlic, salt, peppercorns, thyme, coriander and bay leaves. Sauté to a golden brown.

4.   Add tomato paste and cook for two minutes. Deglaze with white wine.

5.   Add beef and bones to pot then fill with water up to max fill line.

6.   Place lid on cooker, lock the lid and switch the pressure valve to CLOSED.

7.   When timer reaches zero, switch the pressure valve to OPEN. Once all the steam has been released, remove lid.

8.   Pour broth through a strainer with cheesecloth.

9.   Allow broth to cool in the refrigerator overnight, and then skim the fat off the top.

10. Reduce to desired consistency and season to taste.

60

Minutes Under
Pressure

**Yields 2 - 3
Quarts**

Ingredients

4 lbs. beef bones, beef shank, ox tail or short rib

2 medium onions, chopped

3 tbsp. olive oil

3 carrots, chopped

3 stalks of celery, chopped

5 cloves of garlic

¼ oz. dried porcini mushroom

2 tbsp. whole black peppercorns

3 bay leaves

1 tbsp. kosher salt

½ bunch of fresh thyme

2 tbsp. tomato paste

1 cup red wine

3 quarts cold water

Beef Broth

Directions

1.   Add oil to the inner pot and push the CHICKEN/MEAT button (or brown/sauté mode).

2.   Season beef and bones generously with salt and pepper, once the oil is hot, then sear to a deep brown. Remove and set aside.

3.   Add onions, carrot, celery, garlic, porcini, thyme, salt, pepper corns and bay leaves. Sauté to a golden brown.

4.   Add tomato paste and cook for one minute. Deglaze with red wine.

5.   Add beef and bones to pot then fill with water up to max fill line.

6.   Place lid on cooker, switch the pressure valve to CLOSED and lock the lid.

7.   Press keep warm/cancel button to reset.

8.   Press the CHICKEN/MEAT button, then press time adjust button and set to 60 minutes (or 60 min. high pressure).

9.   When timer reaches zero, switch the pressure valve to OPEN. Once all the steam has been released, remove the lid.

10. Pour broth through a strainer with cheesecloth.

11. Allow to cool in the refrigerator overnight, then skim the fat off the top.

12. Reduce to desired consistency and re-season.

**Yields 2 - 3
Quarts**

When a recipe calls for fish broth or stock, having your own stored in your freezer is a lifesaver. Plus, it always tastes better than store bought! I love knowing exactly what is in it because it gives me as the cook more control of the overall result of the dish.

Fish Broth

Ingredients

4 lbs. fish heads and bones

2 medium onions, chopped

3 carrots, chopped

3 stalks of celery, chopped

5 cloves of garlic

2 tbsp. whole black peppercorns

2 tsp. whole coriander seed

3 bay leaves

1 tbsp. kosher salt

½ bunch of fresh thyme

1 cup white wine

3 quarts cold water

Directions

1.   Add oil to pot and push CHICKEN/MEAT button then the time adjustment button to reach 40 minutes (40 minutes high pressure).

2.   When the oil is hot, add onions, carrot, celery, garlic, peppercorns, coriander, salt, thyme and bay leaves. Sauté to a golden brown.

3.   Deglaze with white wine.

4.   Add fish to pot then fill with water up to max fill line.

5.   Place lid on cooker, lock the lid and switch the pressure valve to CLOSED.

6.   When timer reaches zero, switch the pressure valve to OPEN. Once all the steam has been released, remove the lid.

7.   Pour broth through a strainer with cheesecloth.

8.   Allow to cool in the refrigerator overnight, then skim fat off the top.

9.   Reduce to desired consistency and season to taste.

10

Minutes Under
Pressure

SERVES 6 - 8

Ingredients

2 lbs. kielbasa, diced

3 tbsp. extra virgin olive oil

1 cup onion, chopped

1 cup carrot, chopped

1 cup celery, chopped

1 head green or Napa cabbage, chopped

3 cloves garlic, chopped

1½ tsp. caraway seed

1½ tsp. fennel seed

2 tbsp. Dijon mustard

6 cups low-sodium chicken stock

½ cup Italian parsley, chopped

¼ cup potato flakes (optional as a thickener—add at the very end and stir)

Salt and pepper to taste

The great thing about kielbasa is that it's already cooked! That means you can bring dinner to the table even faster when you use it. Plus, it's full of flavor and pairs so well with cabbage.

Cabbage Soup with Kielbasa

Directions

1. Press the SOUP/STEW button (or 10 min high pressure).

2. Heat oil in pot and add kielbasa. Brown for 3 minutes.

3. Add onion, carrot, celery, cabbage, garlic, caraway and fennel. Sauté for 5 minutes.

4. Add stock and mustard.

5. Place the lid on the pressure cooker, lock the lid and switch the pressure valve to CLOSED.

6. Once the timer reaches 0, switch the pressure release valve to OPEN. When the steam is completely released, remove the lid.

7. Salt and pepper to taste. Top with fresh parsley.

Eric's Tip: Add your fresh herbs at the end to keep the flavors bright.

Ingredients

2 tbsp. extra virgin olive oil

1 lb. 90/10 ground beef

2 lb. pork/veal mix (meatloaf mix)

1 lb. brisket cut in small ½ in cubes

4 oz. cured spicy chorizo, diced

2 large onions, diced

1 jalapeño, diced

3 large green bell peppers, diced

2 Anaheim peppers, diced

3 garlic cloves, smashed then minced

1 (28 oz.) can chopped tomatoes

1 tbsp. tomato paste

2 cups white wine

2 cups beef stock

1 tbsp. balsamic vinegar

1/8 cup apple cider vinegar

1/8 cup brown mustard

1 tbsp. cumin

1 tsp. coriander

2 tbsp. chili powder

1 tsp. cayenne pepper

¼ cup Blue Agave syrup

6-oz bar high-quality chocolate (at least 70% cocoa)

Salt and pepper to taste

For the Garnish:

½ cup parsley or cilantro, chopped

1 cup shredded cheddar cheese, for garnish

1 cup sour cream, for garnish

I love chili, but I don't always love beans. There is an ongoing culinary debate about whether or not chili should include beans, so I made this one sans the beans. I also added some very dark and delicious chocolate to it. If you are nervous about that, don't be! Lots of Mexican dishes use dark chocolate in a sauce called "mole." I think the dark chocolate adds a layer of complexity to the chili and really smooths it out. Without actually tasting the chocolate, you get the smooth richness that chocolate imparts.

Eric's Dark Chocolate Chili
(hold the beans)

Directions

1. Place the inner pot into the pressure cooker and press the CHICKEN/MEAT button then the cook time selector button once (40 min. high pressure).

2. When the oil is hot, brown all the meats in batches and drain the fat from the inner pot. Set meats aside.

3. Sauté the peppers and onions in olive oil until soft.

4. Add the meat to the onion and pepper mixture.

5. Add all of the remaining ingredients except the chocolate. Stir very well.

6. Place the lid on the pressure cooker, lock the lid and switch the pressure release valve to CLOSED.

7. Once the timer reaches 0, switch the pressure release valve to OPEN. When the steam is completely released, remove the lid.

8. Stir in the chocolate till melted and season to taste.

9. Serve with shredded cheddar cheese, sour cream and chopped parsley or cilantro.

Eric's Tip: For those of you who love beans, feel free to incorporate 1½ cups of dried beans; I always use dried. Make sure to soak them overnight prior to adding them, and follow the directions on the bag. These dried beans must be added and well incorporated just before you put the lid on.

White Turkey Chili

Ingredients

1 cup dried northern beans

4 tbsp. olive oil

1½ lbs. ground turkey

2 cups onion, diced

1½ cups green pepper, diced

1 tbsp. jalapeño, chopped

1 tbsp. garlic, minced

1 tbsp. cumin

1 tsp. dried oregano

6 cups chicken stock

1 cup salsa verde

1 tsp. salt

½ tsp. pepper

4 cups tortilla chips

1 bunch cilantro, chopped

2 fresh limes, cut into wedges

Directions

1.   Place inner pot in cooker.

2.   Add beans and cover with 1 inch of water.

3.   Place the lid on the cooker, lock the lid and switch the pressure valve to CLOSED.

4.   Hit the BEANS/LENTILS button (or high pressure 5 min).

5.   When the timer reaches zero, hit the cancel/keep warm button (or off/cancel button).

6.   Let the pressure in the cooker release naturally without opening the pressure valve.

7.   When pressure has dropped completely, open the lid.

8.   Drain beans and set aside.

9.   Place the inner pot in the cooker.

10. Press the BEANS/LENTILS button then hit the time adjustment button until you reach 10 minutes (or high pressure 10 min).

11. Add the oil and turkey and sauté until no longer pink.

12. Add the beans, onion, green pepper, jalapeño, garlic, cumin, oregano, chicken stock, salsa verde, salt and pepper.

13. Place the lid on the cooker, lock the lid and switch the pressure valve to CLOSED.

14. When timer reaches zero, switch the pressure valve to OPEN. When steam is completely released, open the lid.

15. Serve with tortilla chips, cilantro and lime wedges.

10

Minutes Under Pressure

SERVES 6 - 8

Ingredients

3 tbsp. extra virgin olive oil

2 lbs. lean ground beef

1 cup onion, chopped

1 cup celery, chopped

1 cup parsnips, chopped

1½ cups crimini mushrooms, chopped

2 cloves garlic, chopped

2 tbsp. tomato paste

1 tbsp. soy sauce

1 cup dry red wine

6 cups low-sodium beef broth

1½ cups uncooked pearl barley

1 bouquet garni of parsley, sage, rosemary and thyme

1 tsp. dried rosemary

1 tbsp. dried thyme

½ cup finely chopped fresh parsley for garnish

Salt and pepper to taste

I called out the parsley, sage, rosemary and thyme because once I hear that famous song I can't get it out of my head and sing it all day long...and now, so will you! But seriously, we all know these herbs go deliciously together.

Beef Barley Soup
with Parsley, Sage, Rosemary and Thyme

Directions

1.   Press the SOUP/STEW button on the pressure cooker (high pressure 10 minutes).

2.   Add oil. When the oil is hot, sear the beef for 5 minutes. Remove, drain fat and set aside.

3.   Add onion, carrot, celery, parsnips, mushrooms and garlic. Sauté vegetables for 5 minutes.

4.   Stir in the tomato paste, soy sauce and then add red wine to deglaze the pot.

5.   Add beef back into pot along with barley, bouquet garni, beef broth, rosemary and thyme.

6.   Place the lid on the cooker, lock the lid and switch the pressure valve to CLOSED.

7.   Once the timer reaches 0, switch the pressure valve open. When the steam is completely released, remove the lid.

8.   Simmer the soup for an extra 10 minutes for a more concentrated flavor. To do this, simply press the SOUP/STEW button (or brown/sauté button) with the lid off at the end of the cooking process. Then press the warm button to keep your soup warm until you are ready to enjoy.

9.   Remove the bouquet garni. Stir well. Salt and pepper to taste. Top with fresh parsley.

Eric's Tip: As with most soups, this soup is even better the next day. Consider cooking it a day ahead.

Note: A "Bouquet Garni" is a grouping of fresh herb sprigs tied together with twine and removed from the pot before consumption.

25

10 Minutes Under Pressure

SERVES 6

Ingredients

5 tsp. extra virgin olive oil

2 lbs. chicken breast, diced into ½-inch pieces

2 cups celery, chopped

2 cups carrot, chopped

1 pinch each salt and pepper

1 cup Buffalo wing sauce

5 cups low-sodium chicken stock

¾ cup half & half

¼ cup potato flakes (for thickening)

Crumbled bleu cheese for garnish

Crusty bread (optional)

I love the taste of Buffalo sauce. Once you have a craving for it, you must act on it! This is simply a play on the classic. It's full of flavor and makes everyone smile.

Buffalo Chicken Soup

Directions

1.   Place inner pot in the pressure cooker. Press the SOUP/STEW button to reach 10 minutes (10 minutes high pressure).

2.   Add 3 tbsp. olive oil, and when the oil is hot, brown chicken for 5 minutes. Remove chicken and set aside.

3.   Heat 2 tbsp. olive oil in pot, then add the carrot, celery, salt and pepper and sauté for 5 minutes.

4.   Slowly whisk in all liquids except the half & half. Return the browned chicken back to the pot.

5.   Place the lid on the pressure cooker, lock the lid and switch the pressure release valve to CLOSED.

6.   When the timer reads 0, switch the pressure release valve to OPEN. Once the steam has been released, open the lid.

7.   Add salt and pepper to taste and half & half. Stir well and then slowly sprinkle in the potato flakes. If after 2 minutes you would like a thicker result, simply sprinkle in additional potato flakes a little bit at a time.

8.   Garnish with bleu cheese.

Eric's Tip: Add additional cold chopped celery into each bowl for garnish to give a nice crunch to the soup.

5
Minutes Under Pressure

SERVES 6 - 8

Ingredients

2 tbsp. olive oil

1 pound hot sausage, casing removed

1½ cups diced onion

1½ cups diced celery

1½ cup diced carrots

2 tsp. minced garlic

1 tsp. dried rosemary

¼ tsp. cayenne pepper

2 ham hocks

1 cup lentils

6 cups chicken stock

I remember my mom making this soup all the time. When I was a youngster, I detested it! Unfortunately for me, it was one of my dad's all time favorite meals. I had no choice but to adapt. Now I love and make it for my family, and, since "dad" likes it, the kids are trumped!

Ham and Lentil Soup

Directions

1. Place inner pot in cooker.

2. Add the oil and press the BEANS/LENTILS button (or high pressure 5 min.).

3. To the hot oil, add the sausage. Sauté and crumble.

4. Add the onion, celery, carrots, garlic, rosemary, cayenne, ham hocks, lentils and stock.

5. Place the lid on the cooker, lock the lid and switch the pressure valve to CLOSED.

6. When timer reaches 0, switch the pressure valve to OPEN.

7. When steam is completely released, open the lid.

8. Remove ham hocks and let cool.

9. Dice the meat from the ham hocks, and add it back into soup.

Ingredients

4 heads cauliflower,
broken into pieces

2 cups onion, diced

2 tsp. minced garlic

2 tsp. dried thyme

2 tsp. salt

½ tsp. pepper

6 cups vegetable stock

1 cup cream

2 tbsp. chopped chives

Cream of Cauliflower Soup

Directions

1. Place inner pot in cooker.

2. Add cauliflower, onion, garlic, thyme, salt, pepper, and stock.

3. Place the lid on the cooker, lock the lid and switch the pressure valve to CLOSED.

4. Hit the FISH/VEG/STEAM button, and then hit the time adjustment button until it reaches 4 minutes (or high pressure 4 min).

5. When timer reaches 0, switch the pressure valve to OPEN.

6. When steam is completely released, open the lid.

7. In batches and in a blender, puree the soup until smooth.

8. Incorporate the cream and garnish with chives.

Eric's Tip: A general helping of your favorite shredded cheese really brings another dimension to this soup.

Ingredients

3 (16 oz.) bags fresh or frozen Asian stir fry vegetables

1 (8 oz.) bag fresh or frozen shelled edamame

1 Thai chili pepper, sliced thin

2 (32 oz.) containers of Thai ginger broth

1 (13.5 oz.) can of coconut milk

½ lb. angel hair pasta, broken in half

1 cup cilantro leaves, chopped

1 cup basil leaves, chopped

1 cup thinly sliced scallions

Juice of 2 limes (optional)

My wife Jesse studied in Thailand in college, and she still talks about the flavors she loved there. Once you start eating the flavors of Thailand, you start to realize how light and fresh everything tastes. Thai recipes display a great balance of flavors often finished with the right amount of heat. This soup acts as a good introduction to Thai flavors.

Thai Noodle Soup

Directions

1.   Press the SOUP/STEW button (or 10 min high pressure).

2.   Heat oil in pot and add kielbasa. Brown for 3 minutes.

3.   Add onion, carrot, celery, garlic, cabbage, caraway and fennel. Sauté for 5 minutes.

4.   Add stock and mustard.

5.   Place the lid on the pressure cooker, lock the lid and switch the pressure valve to CLOSED.

6.   Once the timer reaches 0, the cooker will automatically switch to keep warm. Switch the pressure release valve to OPEN. When the steam is completely released, remove the lid.

7.   Salt and pepper to taste. Top with fresh parsley.

Eric's Tip: For extra flavor, add a squeeze of fresh lime juice to each bowl before serving.

25
Minutes Under Pressure

SERVES 6 - 8

Chicken and Dumpling Soup

Ingredients

1 tbsp. olive oil

2 whole chickens

1 (48 oz.) container low-sodium chicken broth

1 packet of dry Italian salad dressing seasoning

½ medium onion, minced

3 cloves garlic, minced

2 bay leaves

Salt and pepper

1 egg, beaten well

1 cup flour

1 package Klushki noodles (or your favorite noodle)

Directions

1. Place inner pot in cooker and hit the SOUP/STEW button and then the time adjustment button until you reach 25 minutes (or 25 min high pressure).

2. Add olive oil to bottom of preheated inner pot and quickly brown chickens.

3. Remove chickens and drain oil. Return chicken to inner pot.

4. Add chicken broth, seasoning packet, onion, garlic, bay leaves, salt and pepper.

5. Place the lid on the cooker, lock the lid and switch the pressure valve to CLOSED.

6. Once the timer reaches 0, switch the pressure valve to OPEN. Once all the pressure is released, remove the lid. Remove chicken and set aside.

7. Hit the SOUP/STEW button again, and simmer the broth for 15 minutes (or brown/sauté mode).

8. In the meantime, beat egg in bowl and slowly add flour to egg until it reaches the consistency where it will just stick to a spoon.

9. Drop spoonful's of the flour/egg mixture into the boiling liquid and cook until they pop to the top.

10. Add noodles and stir. Cook according to the time on the package.

11. While noodles are cooking, remove chicken from bones and add chicken to the soup.

12. Incorporate and serve.

Eric's Tip: Add some shakes of hot sauce to each bowl for added punch, if you like.

Ingredients

1½ cups wild rice

2 oz. dried porcini mushrooms, chopped

4½ cups water

1½ cups onion, diced

1½ cups celery, diced

1½ cups carrots, diced

2 large sweet potatoes, peeled and diced into ¼-inch pieces

2 tsp. minced garlic

1½ tsp. dried oregano

2 tsp. salt

½ tsp. pepper

8 cups vegetable stock

2 tbsp. chopped fresh parsley

I have always loved mushrooms—even more so when their flavors get concentrated. Dried Porcini mushrooms are in their own flavor wheelhouse, and their earthy taste can't be beaten.

Dried Porcini Mushroom and Wild Rice Soup

Directions

1. Place inner pot in cooker.

2. Add the wild rice, mushrooms and water. Stir.

3. Place lid on cooker and switch pressure valve to CLOSED.

4. Hit the MEAT/CHICKEN button and then the time adjustment button until you reach 20 minutes (or high pressure 20 min.).

5. When the timer reaches zero, hit the cancel/keep warm button (or off/cancel button).

6. Let the pressure in the cooker release naturally without opening the pressure valve.

7. When the pressure has dropped completely, remove lid.

8. Add the onions, celery, carrots, sweet potatoes, garlic, oregano, salt, pepper and stock.

9. Place the lid on the cooker, lock the lid and switch the pressure valve to CLOSED.

10. Hit the RICE/RISOTTO button (or high pressure for 6 minutes).

11. When the timer reaches zero, switch the pressure release valve to OPEN. Once all the pressure has been released, open the lid.

12. Stir in parsley.

5

Minutes Under Pressure

SERVES 6 - 8

Ingredients

Soup:

2 tbsp. olive oil

1 tsp. minced garlic

4 cups leeks, diced

2 cups celery, diced

2 cups carrots, diced

2 cups green beans, sliced

2 cups zucchini, diced

2 cups yellow squash, diced

2 (14.5 oz.) cans petite-diced tomatoes

6 cups vegetable stock

¾ cup uncooked orzo

1 tsp. salt

½ tsp. pepper

Pesto:

2 tsp. minced garlic

¼ cup sun-dried tomatoes in olive oil

¾ cup packed basil leaves

½ cup extra virgin olive oil

¼ cup water

½ cup grated Parmesan cheese

"Pistou" means "pounded" in the French Provencal language, and here it refers to the process that involves pounding the basil into pesto. Pound this dish with flavor!

Soup au Pistou

Directions

1. Place inner pot in cooker.

2. Hit the BEANS/LENTILS button (high pressure 5 minutes).

3. Add the oil, and when the oil is hot, sauté the garlic for 1 minute.

4. Add the leeks and sauté for 2 minutes.

5. Add the celery, carrots, green beans, zucchini, squash, tomatoes, stock, orzo, salt and pepper.

6. Place the lid on the cooker, lock the lid and switch the valve to CLOSED.

7. While the soup is cooking, make the pesto using the following 6 steps.

8. Add the garlic, sun-dried tomatoes and basil into food processor and puree for 30 seconds.

9. Scrape sides.

10. With processor running slowly drizzle in olive oil.

11. Add water in a slow drizzle.

12. Turn off processor and stir in Parmesan by hand.

13. Salt and pepper to taste.

14. When the timer on the cooker reaches zero, switch the pressure release valve to OPEN. When steam is completely released, open the lid.

15. Stir in pesto.

5
Minutes Under Pressure

SERVES 10

Spicy Corn and Crab Chowder

Ingredients

3 tbsp. oil

1½ lbs. fresh chorizo sausage, casings removed

2 cups onions, diced

2 cups celery, diced

1½ cups green bell pepper

1 lb. potatoes, rough chopped

2 cups fresh or frozen corn

1 tbsp. Old Bay seasoning

2 tsp. minced garlic

6 cups chicken stock

1 tsp. salt

½ tsp. pepper

1 lb. cooked crabmeat

½ cup heavy cream

¼ -½ cup instant potato flakes

Directions

1. Place inner pot in cooker.

2. Press the BEANS/LENTILS button (or high pressure 5 minutes).

3. Add oil, and once the oil is hot, add sausage.

4. Sauté sausage and crumble.

5. Add onion, celery, bell pepper, potatoes, corn, Old Bay, garlic, stock, salt and pepper.

6. Place the lid on the cooker, lock the lid and switch the pressure valve to CLOSED.

7. When the timer reaches 0, switch the pressure valve to OPEN. When steam is completely released, open the lid.

8. Add crabmeat and press the FISH/VEG/STEAM button and, leaving the lid off, bring up to a simmer (or use your brown/sauté mode).

9. After about 5 minutes of simmering, add the cream and potato flakes and hit the cancel/keep warm button (or off/cancel button).

10. Stir and serve.

Eric's Tip: If you can't find fresh chorizo, you can make your own by mixing ground sausage, fresh garlic and lots of smoky paprika.

SERVES 10 - 12

Shrimp and Scallop Bisque

Ingredients

1 ½ lbs. shrimp, peeled, deveined and tail removed

1 ½ lbs. scallops

½ cup carrots, diced

½ cup celery, diced

1 cup onion, diced

½ cup white rice

½ cup sun-dried tomatoes, chopped

½ tsp. paprika

¼ tsp. cayenne pepper

1 bay leaf

½ cup sherry

6 cups seafood stock

3 cups heavy cream

2 tsp. tarragon, chopped

1 ½ tsp. salt

½ tsp. black pepper

Directions

1.   Place inner pot in cooker.

2.   Add the shrimp, scallops, carrots, celery, onion, rice, sun-dried tomatoes, paprika, cayenne pepper, bay leaf, sherry and seafood stock.

3.   Place lid on cooker, lock the lid and switch the pressure valve to CLOSED.

4.   Hit the RICE/RISOTTO button (or high pressure 6 min).

5.   When the timer reaches zero, switch the pressure valve to OPEN. When steam is completely released, open the lid.

6.   In a blender, in batches, purée soup until smooth.

7.   When all of the soup is puréed, stir in cream and tarragon.

8.   Salt and pepper to taste.

Eric's Tip: I always love to add an extra drizzle of sherry when it's in the bowl to add a fragrant punch.

50 Minutes Under Pressure

SERVES 6

Ingredients

2 tbsp. olive oil

2 lbs. pork shoulder, cut into ½-inch cubes

2 cups onions, diced

1 cup Poblano pepper, diced

2 tsp. garlic, minced

1 20 oz. can hominy, drained and rinsed

5 cups chicken stock, divided

1 cup salsa verde

2 tbsp. paprika

1 tbsp. cumin

1 tsp. dried oregano

1 tsp. salt

1 tsp. pepper

Fresh cilantro, chopped for garnish

Cabbage, shredded, for garnish

Avocado, diced for garnish

Red onion, chopped, for garnish

Fresh lime wedges for garnish

Fresh tortilla strips for garnish

This traditional comfort food is the Latin equivalent to "Grandma's chicken soup."

Pozole Guerrero

Directions

1.   Place inner pot in cooker.

2.   Hit the CHICKEN/MEAT button and the time adjustment button to reach 20 minutes (20 minutes high pressure).

3.   Add olive oil. Once the oil is hot, in two batches, brown the pork.

4.   Add all pork back into pot.

5.   Add 1 cup of stock.

6.   Place the lid on the cooker, lock the lid and switch the pressure valve to CLOSED.

7.   When the timer reaches 0, switch the pressure valve to OPEN. When the steam is completely released, open the lid.

8.   Add onion, pepper, garlic, hominy, remaining stock, salsa verde, paprika, cumin, oregano, salt and pepper.

9.   Place the lid on the cooker, lock the lid and switch the pressure valve to CLOSED.

10. Press the CHICKEN/MEAT button and then hit the time adjustment button until you reach 30 minutes (high pressure 30 min.).

11. When timer reaches 0, switch the pressure valve to OPEN. When steam is completely released, open the lid.

12. Serve with garnishes.

45
Minutes Under
Pressure

SERVES 6 - 8

This is a soup that is so easy and tasty you will wonder why you haven't made before or maybe why haven't made it in a while. Hominy is simply maize/field corn that can be picked up in just about any grocery store (usually in the Mexican/ethnic section). You can use dried hominy if you like.

Pozole Verde

Ingredients

3 tbsp. olive oil

4 lbs. pork shoulder,
cut into 2-inch cubes

½ cup beef broth

2 (16 oz.) cans hominy corn,
rinsed and drained

2 cups tomatillo purée
(can substitute salsa verde)

3 cloves garlic, chopped

½ cup roasted green chilies

1 medium onion, chopped

1 tbsp. cumin

2 tbsp. paprika

1 tbsp. dried oregano

2 tsp. salt

1 tsp. pepper

Directions

1.   Push CHICKEN/MEAT button then the time adjustment button to reach 45 minutes (45 min. high pressure).

2.   Add olive oil to the inner pot, and once the oil is hot, sear the pork on all sides.

3.   Add remaining ingredients and place lid on pressure cooker. Lock the lid and switch the pressure valve to CLOSED.

4.   When timer reaches 0, switch the pressure valve to OPEN. Once the steam is released, remove the lid.

5.   Garnish and serve.

Eric's Tip: Garnish with fresh radish, red onion, fresh cilantro, avocado, lime wedge and crispy tortilla strips.

10
Minutes Under
Pressure

SERVES 6 - 8

Ingredients

1½ cups dry cannellini beans

2 tbsp. olive oil

1 lb. Italian sausage,
casing removed

8 cups chopped escarole

2 cups diced onion

2 cups diced carrots

½ cup sun-dried tomatoes,
chopped

2 tsp. minced garlic

½ tsp. crushed red chili flakes

1 tsp. dried thyme

2 tsp. dried oregano

1 tsp. salt

½ tsp. black pepper

8 cups chicken stock

Grated Parmesan cheese

Tuscan White Bean Soup

Directions

1. Place inner pot in cooker.

2. Add beans and cover with an inch of water.

3. Place the lid on the cooker, lock the lid and switch the pressure valve to CLOSED.

4. Press the BEANS/LENTILS button (or high pressure 5 min).

5. When the timer reaches 0, hit the cancel/keep warm button (or off/cancel button).

6. Let the pressure drop in the cooker naturally without opening the pressure valve.

7. When the pressure has dropped completely, remove lid.

8. Drain beans and set aside.

9. Place the inner pot in the cooker.

10. Press the BEANS/LENTILS button (or high pressure 5 min).

11. Add the oil and, when the oil is hot, sauté sausage for about 10 minutes, then crumble the sausage.

12. Add the escarole, onion, carrots, sun-dried tomatoes, garlic, chili flakes, thyme, oregano, salt, pepper and stock.

13. Place the lid on the cooker, lock the lid and switch the pressure valve to CLOSED.

14. When timer reaches 0, switch the pressure valve to OPEN. Once the steam has been released, open the lid.

15. Serve with grated Parmesan cheese.

5

Minutes Under Pressure

SERVES 8

Ingredients

2 tbsp. olive oil

2 lbs. ground beef

2/3 cup white rice

2 cups onions, diced

2 cups green bell peppers, diced

2 tsp. minced garlic

2 (14.5 oz.) cans petite diced tomatoes

2 tbsp. tomato paste

6 cups beef stock

1 tsp. dried oregano

1 tsp. dried basil

1 tsp. salt

½ tsp. pepper

2 tbsp. chopped parsley

Grated Parmesan cheese

Sometimes it's just fun to take a classic and twist it. I loved stuffed peppers, and I love soup! So I figured, why not combine those two elements?

Stuffed Pepper Soup

Directions

1. Place inner pot in cooker.

2. Add oil and press the CHICKEN/MEAT button (or brown/sauté).

3. Once the oil is hot, add the beef and sauté until it's no longer pink.

4. Hit the cancel/keep warm button (or off/cancel button).

5. Drain the fat from the ground beef and return to inner pot.

6. Add the rice, onions, peppers, garlic, tomatoes, tomato paste, stock, oregano, basil, salt and pepper.

7. Place lid on cooker, lock the lid and switch the pressure valve to CLOSED.

8. Hit the BEANS/LENTILS button (or high pressure 5 min.).

9. When the timer reaches 0, switch the pressure valve to OPEN.

10. When steam is completely released, open the lid.

11. Stir in parsley and serve topped with cheese.

Appetizers

Most people would not think of using their pressure cooker to make appetizers. As you will see in this section, pressure cookers are an unbelievable helper to get things done quickly and efficiently. Wings, hummus, and deviled eggs are probably the most popular starter for any party or get-together.

Using the pressure cooker will take a lot of the stress out of entertaining for parties and get-togethers, especially with the new technology. Being able to set the pressure cooker and then walk away will free you up to get all of the other tasks done. Even with my restaurant and catering background it can be difficult to prepare for larger parties. With so many distractions, it's easy to forget what's in the oven or on the stove-top. If your pressure cooker automatically turns off or switches to a warming mode like the Power Pressure Cooker XL, it can really take the pressure off of your entertaining and make hosting less stressful.

6
Minutes Under Pressure

YIELDS 24
halves

Ingredients

1 dozen eggs

1 ½ cups water

¾ cup mayonnaise

¾ cup sweet relish

½ tsp. celery seed

Pinch garlic powder

Salt and pepper

Paprika for garnish

Fresh parsley for garnish

Talk about comfort food--my mom has been making these for me for as long as I can remember. Eggs that come out of the pressure cooker will be the easiest eggs you will ever have the pleasure of peeling. The first time my mom tried this method, I think she cried a little. It's that much easier to peel them!

Noni's Basic Deviled Eggs

Directions

1.   Place eggs on steaming/canning rack. Add 1 ½ cups of water. Place the lid on the cooker, lock the lid and switch the pressure valve to CLOSED.

2.   Press the RICE/RISOTTO button (6 minutes on high pressure).

3.   When the cooker reaches 0, switch the pressure valve to OPEN. Once the steam has been released, open the lid.

4.   Place the eggs in an ice bath until cool enough to handle. For best results, peel the eggs immediately. Cut the eggs in half. Carefully remove yolks to a mixing bowl and set aside whites on a platter.

5.   Mix all ingredients except garnish in a mixing bowl.

6.   Scoop into egg white halves and garnish with paprika and fresh parsley.

Eric's Tip: Just a note about the deviled egg recipes in general. They will all make great egg salads as well.

6
Minutes Under
Pressure

**YIELDS 24
halves**

Bacon Cheddar Jalapeño Deviled Eggs

Ingredients

1 dozen eggs

1½ cups water

½ cup mayonnaise

¼ cup prepared salsa

¼ cup shredded cheddar

1 tbsp. fresh jalapeño, seeded and chopped

2 tsp. fresh lime juice

2 tsp. paprika

2 tsp. fresh cilantro, chopped

¼ cup crispy crumbled bacon

Salt and pepper to taste

Directions

1.   Place eggs on steaming/canning rack. Add 1½ cups of water. Place the lid on the cooker, lock the lid and switch the pressure valve to CLOSED.

2.   Press the RICE/RISOTTO button (6 minutes on high pressure).

3.   When the cooker reaches 0, switch the pressure valve to OPEN. Once the steam has been released, open the lid.

4.   Place the eggs in an ice bath until cool enough to handle. For best results, peel the eggs immediately. Cut the eggs in half. Carefully remove yolks to a mixing bowl and set aside whites on a platter.

5.   Mix yolks with all ingredients and scoop into egg whites.

**YIELDS 24
halves**

Ingredients

1 dozen eggs

1½ cups water

1 dozen shrimp, poached
and peeled

3 tsp. old bay seasoning

1 tbsp. chives chopped

2 tsp. fresh lemon juice

1 tbsp. fresh dill chopped

1 tbsp. whole grain mustard

Salt and pepper to taste

Bay Shrimp Deviled Eggs

Directions

1.   Place eggs on steaming/canning rack. Add 1½ cups of water. Place the lid on the cooker, lock the lid and switch the pressure valve to CLOSED.

2.   Press the RICE/RISOTTO button (6 minutes on high pressure).

3.   When the cooker reaches 0, switch the pressure valve to OPEN. Once the steam has been released, open the lid.

4.   Place the eggs in an ice bath until cool enough to handle. For best results, peel the eggs immediately. Cut the eggs in half. Carefully remove yolks to a mixing bowl and set aside whites on a platter.

5.   Slice shrimp in half lengthwise. Save 12 nice pieces then chop the rest.

6.   Mix yolks, chopped shrimp, old bay, chives, lemon juice, mustard, salt and pepper.

7.   Scoop into egg white halves the garnish with shrimp halves.

**YIELDS 24
halves**

Ingredients

1 dozen eggs

1½ cups water

¼ cup mayonnaise

¼ cup sour cream

4 ounces smoked salmon,
chopped

2 tsp. fresh dill, chopped

1 tsp. lemon zest

1 tsp. fresh lemon juice

1 tbsp. capers

1 tbsp. red onion, chopped

Salt and pepper to taste

Smoked Salmon Deviled Eggs

Directions

1.   Place eggs on steaming/canning rack. Add 1½ cups of water. Place the lid on the cooker, lock the lid and switch the pressure valve to CLOSED.

2.   Press the RICE/RISOTTO button (6 minutes on high pressure).

3.   When the cooker reaches 0, switch the pressure valve to OPEN. Once the steam has been released, open the lid.

4.   Place the eggs in an ice bath until cool enough to handle. For best results, peel the eggs immediately. Cut the eggs in half. Carefully remove yolks to a mixing bowl and set aside whites on a platter.

5.   Mix yolks, mayonnaise, sour cream, salmon, lemon juice, zest. Season with salt and pepper.

6.   Scoop into egg white halves and garnish with capers and onion.

Eric's Tip: If you are on a budget, you can substitute quality canned salmon for the smoked.

6
Minutes Under
Pressure

**YIELDS 24
halves**

Ingredients

1 dozen eggs

1½ cups water

¼ cup mayonnaise

½ ripe avocado, mashed

3 tbsp. blue cheese

1 tsp. Worcestershire

3 tbsp. sundried tomatoes, chopped

1 tbsp. fresh basil, chopped

2 tsp. fresh lemon juice

Crispy crumbles bacon for garnish

Salt and pepper to taste

Cobb-Style Deviled Eggs

Directions

1.   Place eggs on steaming/canning rack. Add 1½ cups of water. Place the lid on the cooker, lock the lid and switch the pressure valve to CLOSED.

2.   Press the RICE/RISOTTO button (6 minutes on high pressure).

3.   When the cooker reaches 0, switch the pressure valve to OPEN. Once the steam has been released, open the lid.

4.   Place the eggs in an ice bath until cool enough to handle. For best results, peel the eggs immediately. Cut the eggs in half. Carefully remove yolks to a mixing bowl and set aside whites on a platter.

5.   Mix yolks with mayonnaise, avocado, bleu cheese, Worcestershire, basil, lemon, salt and pepper.

6.   Scoop into egg white halves and garnish with bacon.

**YIELDS 24
halves**

Ingredients

1 dozen eggs

1½ cups water

¼ cup mayonnaise

¼ cup yogurt

¼ cup sour cream

3 tbsp. crumbled feta cheese

¼ cup cucumber, peeled,
seeded and chopped

1 tbsp. fresh dill

1 tbsp. fresh mint, chopped

Salt and pepper to taste

Greek Deviled Eggs

Directions

1. Place eggs on steaming/canning rack.

2. Add 1½ cups of water. Place the lid on the cooker, lock the lid and switch the pressure valve to CLOSED.

3. Press the RICE/RISOTTO button (6 minutes on high pressure).

4. When the cooker reaches 0, switch the pressure valve to OPEN. Once the steam has been released, open the lid.

5. Place the eggs in an ice bath until cool enough to handle. For best results, peel the eggs immediately. Cut the eggs in half. Carefully remove yolks to a mixing bowl and set aside whites on a platter.

6. Mix yolks with all ingredients, the scoop into egg white halves.

Eric's Tip: All of these deviled egg recipes can easily be doubled.

6
Minutes Under Pressure

YIELDS 24 halves

Ingredients

1 dozen eggs

1½ cups water

1/3 cup mayonnaise

¼ cup sour cream

2 tbsp. prepared horseradish

1 tbsp. fresh chopped parsley

2 tsp. cider vinegar

1 tbsp. chopped shallots

Salt and pepper to taste

Thinly sliced, rare roast beef or flank steak for garnish

Steakhouse-Style Deviled Eggs

Directions

1.   Place eggs on steaming/canning rack. Add 1½ cups of water. Place the lid on the cooker, lock the lid and switch the pressure valve to CLOSED.

2.   Press the RICE/RISOTTO button (6 minutes on high pressure).

3.   When the cooker reaches 0, switch the pressure valve to OPEN. Once the steam has been released, open the lid.

4.   Place the eggs in an ice bath until cool enough to handle. For best results, peel the eggs immediately. Cut the eggs in half. Carefully remove yolks to a mixing bowl and set aside whites on a platter.

5.   Mix yolks with all ingredients, the scoop into egg white halves.

6.   Garnish with roast beef or flank steak.

Eric's Tip: I love to put a shot of Worcestershire on these eggs to bring home that steakhouse flavor.

What can one say about wings but that they are just about the perfect appetizer. The flavor and texture are addictive. I put some fun variations in the book so that you can try some different flavor profiles. Nothing can trump the classic Buffalo, but it is a lot of fun to change it up.

Basic Chicken Wings

Ingredients

2 lbs. chicken wings and drumettes

1 tbsp. olive oil

1 tsp. salt

½ tsp. pepper

1 cup chicken broth

Directions

1.   Press the CHICKEN/MEAT button on the pressure cooker (15 minutes high pressure).

2.   Add oil, salt and pepper to cooker.

3.   Once the oil is hot, add chicken to cooker and stir to coat.

4.   Lightly brown chicken.

5.   Add chicken broth. Place the lid on the cooker, lock the lid and switch the pressure valve to CLOSED.

6.   When the timer reaches 0, switch the pressure valve to OPEN and remove the lid. Next, drain the liquid and add your favorite sauce recipe.

Eric's Tip: **For great Buffalo wings, combine ¾ cup hot sauce and ¼ cup of melted butter and add to the wings in the cooker, tossing to coat the wings just before serving.**

Also, browning the wings prior to pressure cooking them is OPTIONAL. I like the color and flavor better when they have been browned. If you like your wings well done and crispy, simply place them on a baking pan and place them under the oven broiler until desired doneness.

**Makes about
1 cup**

Ingredients

2 tbsp. soy sauce
1 tbsp. brown sugar
1 tbsp. honey
½ tsp. cayenne pepper
½ tsp. paprika
½ tsp. allspice
½ tsp. ground ginger
½ tsp. dried thyme
1 clove garlic, chopped
1 scallion, chopped
1 lime, zested and juiced
1 tbsp. cider vinegar

Jamaican Jerk Wing Sauce

Directions

1. Combine all ingredients.

2. Add to basic chicken wing recipe.

**Makes about
1½ cups**

Ingredients

1 cup sweet chili sauce
1 orange, zested and juiced
1 tbsp. hoisin sauce
1 tbsp. honey
1 tbsp. soy sauce
2 tsp. Chinese 5-spice
1 scallion, chopped
½ tsp. ground ginger
1 tsp. toasted sesame oil
1 tsp. fresh Thai chili, sliced
paper thin

Sticky Spicy Asian Wing Sauce

Directions

1. Combine all ingredients.

2. Add to basic chicken wing recipe.

Ingredients

5 lbs. frozen wings

8 oz. stout beer

1 tbsp. butter

For the sauce:

1 cup prepared yellow mustard

¼ cup Dijon mustard

1 cup apple cider vinegar

½ cup brown sugar

2 tbsp. soy sauce

½ tsp. cayenne pepper

1 tsp. onion powder

1 tsp. cumin

1 tsp. coriander

1 tsp. crushed black pepper

½ tsp. salt

This is my play on a favorite snack. Have you ever had the pretzels that are coated in mustard flavor? I love them; I also love wings. When I made it, I didn't realize until it was done that it tastes a lot like a Carolina BBQ sauce. But then again, what does a Jersey boy like me know about that?

Wings with Beer and Mustard

Directions

1. Prepare the sauce ahead of time by combining everything except the wings, beer and butter in a bowl.

2. Place the inner pot inside the pressure cooker and press the CHICKEN/MEAT button once (for 15 min high pressure).

3. Add the frozen wings, beer and the sauce.

4. Place the lid on the pressure cooker, lock the lid and switch the pressure valve to CLOSED.

5. Once the timer reaches 0, switch the pressure release valve to OPEN. Once the steam has been released, remove the lid.

6. With a slotted spoon, remove the wings to a serving bowl.

7. Add the butter to the sauce in the pot and stir well until melted. Pour sauce over wings and serve.

Eric's Tip: For the wings, using fresh or frozen wings doesn't change the timing.

60
Minutes Under
Pressure

YIELDS 6 cups

What a great and healthy snack hummus is! I have a few variations in the book that I hope you will try. I dip carrots or celery in hummus all of the time for a crunchy, guilt-free snack. I always try to make sure it's on the after school snack list as well.

Hummus Base Recipe

Ingredients

1 lb. dried garbanzo beans, sorted and rinsed

9 cups water

1 tbsp. kosher salt

¾ cup tahini

1 tbsp. chopped garlic

2 tbsp. fresh lemon juice

1 tbsp. ground cumin

¼ cup extra virgin olive oil

2 tsp. kosher salt

Fresh ground pepper to taste

Directions

1. Place the inner pot in cooker, then add the garbanzos, water and salt.

2. Push CHICKEN/MEAT button then the time adjustment button until you reach 60 min. (or high for 60 min).

3. Place the lid on the pressure cooker, lock the lid and switch the pressure valve to CLOSED.

4. When timer reaches 0, switch the pressure valve to OPEN. Once the steam is released, remove the lid.

5. Scoop out garbanzos and reserve cooking water. Using a stick blender or food processor, purée garbanzos with tahini, garlic, lemon juice, cumin, salt, pepper and olive oil. Use the reserved liquid to adjust consistency close to a thick pancake batter. Once cool, the hummus will thicken more.

YIELDS 6 cups

Sriracha Cilantro Hummus

Ingredients

1 lb. dried garbanzo beans, sorted and rinsed

9 cups water

¾ cup tahini

1 tbsp. chopped garlic

1 tbsp. ground cumin

¼ cup extra virgin olive oil

9 tbsp. Sriracha sauce

6 tbsp. fresh cilantro, chopped

3 limes, zest chopped and juiced

2 tsp. kosher salt

Fresh ground pepper to taste

Directions

1.   Place the inner pot in cooker, then add the garbanzos, water and salt.

2.   Push CHICKEN/MEAT button then the time adjustment button until you reach 60 min. (or high for 60 min). Place the lid on the pressure cooker, lock the lid and switch the pressure valve to CLOSED.

3.   When timer reaches 0, switch the pressure valve to OPEN. Once the steam is released, remove the lid.

4.   Scoop out garbanzos and reserve cooking water. Using a stick blender or food processor, purée garbanzos with tahini, garlic, lime juice, cumin, salt, pepper, Sriracha and olive oil. Stir in the fresh cilantro. Use the reserved liquid to adjust consistency close to a thick pancake batter. Once cool, the hummus will thicken more.

Kale and spinach are touted as super foods for their nutrient rich qualities. I just call them great tasting foods! Using Kale is a great way to go when you are entertaining because it holds up so well. Most greens wilt almost immediately after dressing them. Kale can be dressed ahead of time and will be waiting for you when dinner is ready. The lemon flavor along with the nutrients in the kale and the low calorie goodness of hummus makes this a real winner.

Lemon Kale Hummus

Ingredients

1 lb. dried garbanzo beans, sorted and rinsed

9 cups water

1 tbsp. kosher salt

¾ cup tahini

1 tbsp. chopped garlic

1 tbsp. ground cumin

¼ cup extra virgin olive oil

3 lemons, zest chopped and juiced

1½ cups kale, sautéed and chopped

2 tsp. kosher salt

4 tsp. fresh ground black pepper

Directions

1.   Place the inner pot in cooker, then add the garbanzos, water and salt.

2.   Push CHICKEN/MEAT button then the time adjustment button until you reach 60 min. (or high for 60 min). Place the lid on the pressure cooker, lock the lid and switch the pressure valve to CLOSED.

3.   When timer reaches 0, switch the pressure valve to OPEN. Once the steam is released, remove the lid.

4.   Scoop out garbanzos and reserve cooking water. Using a stick blender or food processor, purée garbanzos with tahini, garlic, lemon juice, cumin, salt, pepper and olive oil. Stir in the kale. Use the reserved liquid to adjust consistency close to a thick pancake batter. Once cool, the hummus will thicken more.

Eric's Tip: **You can substitute any leafy green vegetable such as spinach or Swiss chard. The key is to use what is fresh at the market.**

60
Minutes Under
Pressure

YIELDS 6 cups

Ingredients

1 lb. dried garbanzo beans,
sorted and rinsed

9 cups water

1 tbsp. kosher salt

¾ cup tahini

1 tbsp. chopped garlic

2 tbsp. fresh lemon juice

1 tbsp. ground cumin

¼ cup extra virgin olive oil

3 tbsp. prepared basil pesto

6 tbsp. chopped sundried
tomato in olive oil

¾ cup shredded Pecorino
Romano cheese

2 tsp. kosher salt

Fresh ground pepper to taste

1 cup pine nuts, toasted for
garnish

Tuscan Hummus

Directions

1.   Place the inner pot in cooker, then add the garbanzos, water and salt.

2.   Push CHICKEN/MEAT button then the time adjustment button until you reach 60 min. (or high for 60 min). Place the lid on the pressure cooker, lock the lid and switch the pressure valve to CLOSED.

3.   When timer reaches 0, switch the pressure valve to OPEN. Once the steam is released, remove the lid.

4.   Scoop out garbanzos and reserve cooking water. Using a stick blender or food processor, purée garbanzos with tahini, garlic, lemon juice, cumin, salt, pepper and olive oil. Stir in the pesto, sundried tomatoes, and Romano cheese. Use the reserved liquid to adjust consistency close to a thick pancake batter. Once cool, the hummus will thicken more.

5.   Garnish with pine nuts.

YIELDS 6 cups

Ingredients

1 lb. dried garbanzo beans, sorted and rinsed

9 cups water

1 tbsp. kosher salt

¾ cup tahini

1 tbsp. chopped garlic

2 tbsp. fresh lemon juice

1 tbsp. ground cumin

¼ cup extra virgin olive oil

3 (14 oz.) cans artichoke hearts, drained and small chopped

1½ cups shredded Gruyere cheese

6 tsp. herbs de province

2 tsp. kosher salt

Fresh ground pepper to taste

1 cup toasted hazelnuts, chopped for garnish

South of France Hummus

Directions

1. Place the inner pot in cooker, then add the garbanzos, water and salt.

2. Push CHICKEN/MEAT button then the time adjustment button until you reach 60 min. (or high for 60 min). Place the lid on the pressure cooker, lock the lid and switch the pressure valve to CLOSED.

3. When timer reaches 0, switch the pressure valve to OPEN. Once the steam is released, remove the lid.

4. Scoop out garbanzos and reserve cooking water. Using a stick blender or food processor, puree garbanzos with tahini, garlic, lemon juice, cumin, salt, pepper and olive oil. Incorporate the artichoke hearts, Gruyere cheese, and herbs de province. Use the reserved liquid to adjust consistency close to a thick pancake batter. Once cool, the hummus will thicken more.

5. Garnish with chopped hazelnuts.

60

Minutes Under Pressure

YIELDS 6 cups

Ingredients

1 lb. dried garbanzo beans, sorted and rinsed

9 cups water

1 tbsp. kosher salt

¾ cup tahini

1 tbsp. chopped garlic

2 tbsp. fresh lemon juice

1 tbsp. ground cumin

¼ cup extra virgin olive oil

¾ cup buffalo sauce

¾ cup celery, small diced

¾ cup carrots, small diced

2 tsp. kosher salt

Fresh ground pepper to taste

1 cup crumbled bleu cheese for garnish

Game Day Hummus

Directions

1.   Place the inner pot in cooker, then add garbanzos, water and salt.

2.   Push CHICKEN/MEAT button then the time adjustment button until you reach 60 min. (or high for 60 min). Place the lid on the pressure cooker, lock the lid and switch the pressure valve to CLOSED.

3.   When timer reaches 0, switch the pressure valve to OPEN. Once the steam is released, remove the lid.

4.   Scoop out garbanzos and reserve cooking water. Using a stick blender or food processor, puree garbanzos with tahini, garlic, lemon juice, cumin, salt, pepper and olive oil.

5.   Stir in the buffalo sauce, celery and carrots.

6.   Use the reserved liquid to adjust consistency close to a thick pancake batter. Once cool, the hummus will thicken more.

7.   Garnish with crumbled bleu cheese.

60

Minutes Under Pressure

YIELDS 6 cups

Ingredients

1 lb. dried garbanzo beans, sorted and rinsed

9 cups water

1 tbsp. kosher salt

¾ cup tahini

1 tbsp. chopped garlic

2 tbsp. fresh lemon juice

1 tbsp. ground cumin

¼ cup extra virgin olive oil

1½ cup dried figs, small diced

1½ tsp. dried oregano

¾ cup sunflower seeds

2 tsp. kosher salt

Fresh ground pepper to taste

¾ cup crumbled feta for garnish

Balsamic syrup for drizzle on top

Mediterranean Hummus

Directions

1. Place the inner pot in cooker, then add the garbanzos, water and salt.

2. Push CHICKEN/MEAT button then the time adjustment button until you reach 60 min. (or high for 60 min). Place the lid on the pressure cooker, lock the lid and switch the pressure valve to CLOSED.

3. When timer reaches 0, switch the pressure valve to OPEN. Once the steam is released, remove the lid.

4. Scoop out garbanzos and reserve cooking water. Using a stick blender or food processor, purée garbanzos with tahini, garlic, lemon juice, cumin, salt, pepper and olive oil. Incorporate the figs, oregano and sunflower seeds. Use the reserved liquid to adjust consistency close to a thick pancake batter. Once cool, the hummus will thicken more.

5. Garnish with crumbled feta and finish with balsamic drizzle.

Eric's Tip: This recipe can double as an awesome sandwich or wrap condiment instead of using a traditional mayonnaise.

Pasta and Rice

In this section you will be amazed at how easy cooking pasta and rice can be. If you have the Power Pressure Cooker, it's especially easy thanks to many pre-sets, but it's also simple in any pressure cooker once you know the timing and the liquid ratios. Growing up with an Italian mom, it wasn't easy for me to let go and cook pasta in this manner. Not because I didn't believe it would work, but to step away from a traditional method was a leap of faith. What is most striking is the ease and time savings, not just cooking times but in cleanup time. There is no need for colanders and no frustration of boil overs. When cooking pasta, I have found that no matter what the recipe calls for in the way of liquid, you must make sure that the pasta is completely covered. It's ok if you need to add a bit more liquid to completely cover whatever type of pasta you are using. I have found that the thicker pastas (penne, rotini, etc.) work much better than the thinner, more fragile types (angel hair).

Try cooking the pasta in broth or stock instead of water, or even with cheese and pasta sauce! The same goes for rice. Now you won't need to use the more expensive fast cooking rice because it's so easy and efficient to cook rice quickly in the pressure cooker. In many cases you can now cook your rice at the same time and in the same pot as your main course. The rice will absorb the flavors and give you a better end result, thanks to cooking it under pressure. Again, it's not just about saving time, but enhancing flavors and making true one pot cooking a reality.

Penang Curry Chicken Risotto

Ingredients

3 tbsp. olive oil

2 lbs. boneless skinless chicken breast, ½-inch diced

1 medium onion, diced

1 clove garlic, chopped

2 tbsp. fresh ginger, chopped

3 tbsp. Penang red curry paste

2 cups Arborio rice

1 can unsweetened coconut milk

3 cups chicken stock

1 fresh jalapeño, seeded and chopped

¼ cup fresh cilantro, chopped

¼ cup fresh basil, chopped

1 tsp. salt

2 tsp. black pepper

1 fresh lime, sliced into wedges

Directions

1.   Press RICE/RISOTTO button and press time adjustment button to reach 8 minutes (8 min. high pressure).

2.   Add oil, and, when the oil is hot, sauté chicken and onions for 5 minutes.

3.   Add garlic, ginger, curry paste, Arborio rice and sauté for another 2 minutes.

4.   Add chicken stock and coconut milk.

5.   Place the lid on the cooker, lock the lid, and switch the pressure valve to CLOSED.

6.   When timer reaches 0, switch the pressure valve to OPEN, and, once all the steam has been released, open the lid.

7.   Stir in cilantro, basil, jalapeno, salt and pepper. Garnish with lime wedges.

Eric's Tip: If Thai curry is not available, any pre-made Indian curry sauce can be used for an equally delicious flavor profile.

Shrimp Scampi Risotto

Ingredients

1 lb. peeled and deveined shrimp, diced

3 tbsp. olive oil

2 cups Arborio rice

¼ lb. bacon, chopped

¼ cup shallots, diced

3 cups vegetable or shellfish stock

1 cup white wine

3 cloves garlic, chopped

1/3 cup Italian flat leaf parsley, chopped

2 cup frozen peas, thawed

¼ cup goat cheese

2 tsp. Old Bay seasoning

1 tsp. salt

2 tsp. black pepper

1 lemon, zested and juiced

Directions

1. Press RICE/RISOTTO button and push time adjustment to reach 6 minutes (or high pressure 6 min).

2. Add olive oil to the pot. When the oil is hot, sauté bacon, shrimp, shallots and garlic for 3 minutes.

3. Add Arborio rice and sauté for another 2 minutes.

4. Add wine, Old Bay seasoning, salt, pepper and cook for another 2 minutes.

5. Add stock, lemon juice.

6. Place the lid on cooker, and lock the lid into place. Switch the pressure release valve to CLOSED.

7. When timer reaches 0, switch the pressure valve to OPEN and remove the lid.

8. Stir in parsley, peas, goat cheese, lemon juice and then top with lemon zest.

Eric's Tip: I love taking the leftovers the next day and forming them into patties, then sautéing them to a crispy brown in a non-stick skillet.

**SERVES
ABOUT 6**

Ingredients

3 tbsp. olive oil

2 lbs. hot sausage
(casing removed/crumbled)

2 cups Arborio Rice

1½ cups onion, chopped

3 cups beef stock

1 cup red wine

1 tbsp. garlic, minced

2 tsp. dried thyme

Juice of one lemon

4 oz. sour cream

1 cup Parmesan cheese

1 tbsp. butter

½ cup milk

Zest of 1 lemon

Salt and pepper to taste

Why do I cook with a lot of sausage? Because sausage is GOOD! There is so much flavor in sausage, so it makes cooking tasty dishes easy. Take a dish like risotto. You have the power of the pressure cooker to make that usually laborious task easy and fast. Your family or guests will enjoy the comforting texture and delicious taste of homemade risotto in minutes.

Risotto with Spicy Sausage

Directions

1.   Place the inner pot in the cooker and pour the oil in the inner pot. Press the RICE/RISOTTO button. Press the time adjustment to reach 8 min. (8 min. high pressure).

2.   When the oil is hot, place the sausage in the pot, stirring occasionally while browning.

3.   Pour out and discard excess fat. Add the rice and onions and sauté for 2 minutes.

4.   Add the stock, wine, garlic, thyme and lemon juice. Stir.

5.   Place the lid on the pressure cooker, lock the lid and switch the pressure release valve to CLOSED.

6.   Once the timer reaches 0, switch the pressure release valve to OPEN. When the steam is completely released, remove the lid.

7.   Add the remaining ingredients and incorporate well.

Eric's Tip: **This works well as an appetizer or as a dinner. Add some extra beef stock before reheating leftovers.**

6
Minutes Under
Pressure

**SERVES
ABOUT 10**

Ingredients

2 tbsp. oil

2 lbs. Italian sausage, casings removed

3 tsp. garlic, minced

1½ cups medium onion, diced

2 red peppers, medium diced

1 green pepper, medium diced

2½ cups Arborio rice

½ cup white wine

1 (14.5 oz.) can petite diced tomatoes

6½ cups chicken stock

1 tsp. dried oregano

1 tsp. dried basil

2 tsp. salt

½ tsp. black pepper

3 tbsp. butter

¾ cup Parmesan cheese

Sausage, Pepper and Onion Risotto

Directions

1. Place the inner pot into the cooker.

2. Hit the RICE/RISOTTO button (or 6 min. high pressure).

3. Add oil. When the oil is heated, in two batches brown and crumble sausage.

4. Remove sausage and set aside.

5. Add garlic, onions and peppers and sauté for 2 minutes.

6. Add the rice and stir to coat the rice.

7. Add the wine, tomatoes, stock, oregano, basil, salt and pepper.

8. Stir well.

9. Place the lid on the cooker, lock the lid and switch the pressure valve to CLOSED.

10. When the timer reaches 0, switch the pressure valve to OPEN.

11. When the steam is completely released, open the lid.

12. Stir in butter and cheese.

13. Serve.

6
Minutes Under
Pressure

SERVES 8 – 10

Ingredients

9 ounces thinly sliced pancetta, diced

3 tsp. minced garlic

1½ cup onion, small diced

1½ pound sliced cremini mushrooms

3 cups arborio rice

¾ cup white wine

6 cups chicken stock

1 tsp. dried thyme

2 tsp. salt

½ tsp. pepper

2 tbsp. butter

2½ cups frozen peas

¾ cup grated Parmesan cheese

Mushroom, Pancetta and Pea Risotto

Directions

1. Place the inner pot into the cooker, and press the RICE/RISOTTO button (or 6 min. high pressure).

2. When the pot is hot, add the pancetta and cook until crispy.

3. Add garlic, onions and mushrooms, and sauté for 5 minutes.

4. Add the rice and stir to coat the rice.

5. Add the wine, stock, thyme, salt and pepper, and stir.

6. Place the lid on the cooker, lock the lid and switch the pressure valve to CLOSED.

7. When the timer reaches 0, switch the pressure valve to OPEN.

8. When the steam is completely released, open lid.

9. Stir in butter, peas and cheese.

10. Serve.

Tuscan Risotto

Ingredients

3 tbsp. olive oil

¼ pound pancetta, diced

¼ pound speck, diced

1 medium onion, diced

1 clove garlic chopped

1½ ounces dried porcini mushrooms

2 cups Arborio rice

1 cup white wine

3 cups beef stock

1 tsp. salt

2 tsp. black pepper

¼ cup marinated sundried tomato, chopped

1 can artichoke hearts, chopped

½ cup Gorgonzola crumbles

½ cup Parmesan cheese

¼ cup fresh basil, chopped

1 cup asparagus, blanched and sliced

Directions

1.   Press the RICE/RISOTTO button and set time for 8 minutes (or 8 min. high pressure). Once the pot is hot, add the oil.

2.   Once the oil is hot, add pancetta, speck, onion, garlic, porcini mushroom and sauté for 3 minutes.

3.   Add Arborio rice and sauté for another 2 minutes.

4.   Add wine and simmer for another 2 minutes.

5.   Add beef stock, salt, pepper and sundried tomato.

6.   Place lid on cooker, lock the lid and switch the pressure release valve to CLOSED.

7.   When timer reaches 0, switch the pressure valve to OPEN and remove lid.

8.   Stir in artichokes, Gorgonzola, Parmesan, basil and asparagus.

5 Minutes Under Pressure

SERVES 8 – 10

Ingredients

1½ lbs. bowtie pasta

½ lb. cooked chicken, shredded or diced

1 (14.5 oz.) can petite diced tomatoes

1 (16 oz.) bag chopped frozen spinach

2 cups cream starter or jarred Alfredo sauce

5 cups chicken stock

2 tsp. minced garlic

1 tsp. dried oregano

1½ tsp. dried basil

2 tsp. salt

½ tsp. black pepper

2 cups shredded mozzarella

Grated Parmesan

"Toss and Go" Chicken Florentine Bowtie Pasta

Directions

1. Place inner pot in cooker.

2. Add the pasta, chicken, tomatoes, spinach, cream starter or Alfredo sauce, stock, garlic, oregano, basil, salt and pepper.

3. Stir together.

4. Place lid on the cooker, lock the lid and switch the pressure valve to CLOSED.

5. Press the BEANS/LENTILS button (high pressure 5 min).

6. When the timer reaches 0, switch the pressure valve to OPEN.

7. When steam is completely released, open the lid.

8. Stir in mozzarella and serve with Parmesan cheese.

Eric's Tip: Replace 1 cup of the Alfredo sauce with 1 cup of tomato sauce to make a delicious rose sauce instead.

SERVES 8 – 10

Philly Cheesesteak Stroganoff

Ingredients

8 cups beef stock, divided

2 (21 oz.) boxes frozen beefsteak sandwich meat, broken in large pieces

2 tbsp. oil

2 tsp. minced garlic

3 cups diced onions

3 cups diced peppers

1 lb. sliced mushrooms

2 (10.5 oz.) cans cream of mushroom soup

1½ lbs. fusilli pasta

1 tbsp. Worcestershire sauce

2 tsp. salt

1 tsp. black pepper

2 cups shredded provolone cheese

1 cup sour cream

Directions

1. Place inner pot in cooker.

2. Add 1.5 cups of stock and the sandwich meat.

3. Place lid on the cooker, lock the lid and switch the pressure valve to CLOSED.

4. Hit the BEANS/LENTILS button (or high pressure 5 min).

5. When the timer reaches 0, switch the pressure valve to OPEN. Once the pressure has been released, open the lid.

6. Stir sandwich meat to break it up.

7. Drain meat and set aside.

8. Place inner pot in cooker. Add oil.

9. Hit LENTILS/BEANS button (or brown/sauté mode).

10. Add garlic, onions, peppers and mushrooms and sauté for about 10 minutes.

11. Add the remaining 6.5 cups of beef stock, cream of mushroom soup, fusilli pasta, Worcestershire sauce, salt, and pepper.

12. Place the lid on the cooker and switch the pressure valve to CLOSED. Timer will be set for 5 minutes high pressure.

13. When the timer reaches 0, switch the pressure valve to OPEN. When steam is completely released, open lid.

14. Stir in the meat, provolone and sour cream.

Eric's Tip: Serve this (as we say in Philly) "wit" or "witout" ketchup or cheese whiz!

Ingredients

2 tbsp. olive oil

2 cups diced onions

2 tsp. minced garlic

1½ lbs. penne

3 (6.5 oz.) cans chopped clams

2 (15 oz.) cans white clam sauce

2 (8 ounce) bottles clam juice

1 cup white wine

1 tsp. dried oregano

1 tsp. salt

½ tsp. pepper

½ cup chopped fresh parsley

Grated Parmesan for garnish

Penne with White Clam Sauce

Directions

1. Place inner pot in cooker.

2. Add the olive oil.

3. Hit the BEANS/LENTILS button (high pressure 5 min).

4. Add the onions and garlic and sauté for about 5 minutes.

5. Add the penne, chopped clams, clam sauce, clam juice, wine, oregano, salt and pepper.

6. Place the lid on the cooker, lock the lid and switch the pressure valve to CLOSED.

7. When timer reaches 0, switch the pressure valve to OPEN.

8. When steam is completely released, open lid.

9. Stir in fresh parsley.

10. Serve with grated Parmesan.

Eric's Tip: Don't forget the grilled crusty bread to soak up all that awesome sauce!

5
Minutes Under
Pressure

SERVES 8 – 10

"Toss and Go" Bruschetta Pasta

Ingredients

2 lbs. penne

2 (14.5 oz.) cans petite-diced tomatoes

1½ tbsp. minced garlic

½ tsp. crushed red pepper

2 tsp. salt

½ tsp. pepper

8 cups vegetable stock

1 cup chopped fresh basil

8 ounces fresh mozzarella, ¼-inch diced

Directions

1. Place inner pot in cooker.

2. Add penne, tomatoes, garlic, red pepper, salt, pepper and stock.

3. Stir ingredients.

4. Place lid on cooker, lock the lid and switch pressure valve to CLOSED.

5. Hit the BEANS/LENTILS button (or high pressure 5 min).

6. When the timer reaches zero, hit the cancel/keep warm button (or off/cxl button).

7. Switch the pressure valve to OPEN.

8. When steam is completely released, open lid.

9. Stir in basil and mozzarella.

Ingredients

3 tbsp. olive oil

1½ lbs. thick-cut bacon, chopped

1 lb. short pasta, such as fusilli

4 cups water

4 cups grape tomatoes, halved

1 cup celery, diced

½ cup red onion, diced

1 tbsp. fresh dill, chopped

2 tbsp. capers

1 large head of romaine lettuce

1 cup mayonnaise

¾ cup ranch dressing

1/3 cup Gorgonzola crumbles

Fresh ground black pepper

Salt to taste

BLT Pasta Salad

Directions

1.   Push CHICKEN/MEAT button. Add oil to the inner pot (brown/sauté mode).

2.   Add bacon, and cook until crispy. Drain and set aside.

3.   Pour out excess bacon fat, then add water and pasta.

4.   Push RICE/RISOTTO button and set time for 5 minutes (or 5 min. high pressure).

5.   When timer reaches 0, switch the pressure valve to OPEN and, once all the pressure has been released, remove lid.

6.   Drain pasta and cool thoroughly in fridge.

7.   Slice romaine in ½-inch strips then wash and dry thoroughly.

8.   Combine all ingredients, then garnish with crispy bacon bits on top of salad.

"Pasta Carbonara" is a family favorite of mine, and we refer to it as "Italian bacon and eggs." In this recipe I use bacon, but most of the time I use speck. Speck is flavored, smoked, cured ham usually diced small. I like it because it has tons of flavor and is easier to brown than bacon. Pasta Carbonara may just become one of your family's staples as well!

Cam Cam's Fusilli Carbonara

Ingredients

1 lb. bacon, cut in ½-inch pieces

2 cloves garlic, minced

2 tbsp. olive oil

1 lb. fusilli (or penne)

4 cups water

2 cups Parmesan, grated (plus extra for garnish)

3 eggs plus 4 yolks

1 tbsp. fresh crushed black pepper

Salt and pepper to taste

½ cup chopped parsley for garnish

Directions

1. Place the inner pot in the pressure cooker and add bacon. Press the RICE/RISOTTO button (6 min. high pressure).

2. Once the inner pot is hot, sauté the bacon until almost crispy (you will need to drain the fat halfway through to achieve crispiness). Once bacon is cooked, then add garlic. Stir. Sauté for 1 minute more, then remove and set aside retaining whatever is left of the bacon fat.

3. Add olive oil to the inner pot. Add the pasta and stir for one minute. Add the water. Make sure the water JUST barely covers the pasta. It's okay to add more water if needed.

4. Place the lid on the pressure cooker and lock. Turn the pressure release valve to the CLOSED.

5. While the pasta is cooking, whisk the eggs in a bowl until beaten. Add the Parmesan and incorporate well with the whisk. Add crushed pepper.

6. Once the timer reaches 0, switch the pressure release valve to OPEN. Once the steam has been released, open the lid.

7. Stir the pasta, and then fold in the bacon/garlic mixture. Next, fold in the egg mixture. Add salt and pepper to taste and garnish with fresh parsley.

8. Serve immediately.

Eric's Tip: You can replace the bacon with chicken or turkey sausage for a healthier twist.

8

Minutes Under
Pressure

SERVES 6 – 8

Ingredients

3 tbsp. olive oil

1 lb. chicken thighs, diced

½ lb. chorizo, sliced

1 lb. mussels, cleaned

½ lb. shrimp, peeled and deveined

1 cup roasted red pepper, diced

1 cup yellow onion, diced

3 cloves garlic, chopped

2 cups short grain rice

5 cups chicken broth

½ cup white wine

1 pinch saffron

½ tsp. red pepper flake

1 tsp. turmeric

1 tsp. paprika

1 cup frozen peas, thawed

Italian parsley, chopped for garnish

Paella Tradicional

Directions

1.   Add oil to the inn pot and press the RICE/RISOTTO button and adjust time for 8 minutes (8 min. high pressure).

2.   Once the oil is hot, add chicken, chorizo, onions and garlic, and brown for about 8 minutes.

3.   Add roasted pepper, saffron, paprika, turmeric and rice. Stir and sauté for another 2 minutes.

4.   Deglaze with wine, then add chicken stock and stir well.

5.   Add shrimp then mussels. Lock lid into place and CLOSE the pressure valve.

6.   When the timer reaches 0, switch the pressure valve to OPEN. Once the steam has been released, open the lid.

7.   Spoon out mussels, then stir in peas and parsley.

7
Minutes Under Pressure

SERVES 6 – 8

This hearty dish is a fun replacement for your usual chili standard on game day!

Three Bean Pasta with Sausage and Pesto

Ingredients

3 tbsp. olive oil

1 lb. sausage, removed from casing

1 medium onion chopped

1 cup celery, chopped

1 cup carrots, chopped

3 cups kale or escarole, chopped

3 cloves garlic, chopped

1 tsp. red pepper flakes

6 cups chicken broth

1 (28 oz.) can diced tomato

1 (14 oz.) can kidney beans, rinsed and drained

1 (14 oz.) can cannellini beans, rinsed and drained

1 (14 oz.) can garbanzo beans, rinsed and drained

1 lb. box of rigatoni pasta

3 tbsp. prepared pesto sauce

¼ cup shredded Parmesan cheese

Directions

1.   Press RICE/RISOTTO button and press the time adjustment button to reach 7 minutes (7 min. high pressure).

2.   When the inner pot is hot, brown the sausage for 5 minutes, breaking it up as it cooks. Drain the fats.

3.   Add onions, celery, carrots, kale, and garlic and red pepper flake. Sauté for 3 minutes until greens are wilted.

4.   Add broth, tomato, beans and stir.

5.   Gently fold in uncooked pasta.

6.   Place lid on cooker, lock the lid and switch the pressure valve to CLOSED.

7.   When timer reaches 0, switch the pressure valve to OPEN. Once the steam is released, remove the lid.

8.   Stir in pesto sauce and Parmesan cheese.

35
Minutes Under Pressure

SERVES 4 – 6

Veal and Mushroom Ragout

Ingredients

3-4 lbs. veal stew meat, cubed

3 tbsp. olive oil

4 shallots, chopped

3 cloves garlic, chopped

3 tbsp. tomato paste

2 oz. dried porcini mushrooms

½ lb. Crimini mushrooms, sliced

½ lb. Shitake mushrooms, sliced

2 cups pearl onions

1 can cannellini beans, rinsed and drained

½ cup port wine

¼ cup brandy

1 cup beef broth

1/3 cup fresh Italian parsley, chopped

Salt and pepper to taste

½ cup potato flakes

Directions

1.   Season veal cubes with salt and pepper.

2.   Add oil to the inner pot, then press the CHICKEN/MEAT button and press the time adjustment button to reach 35 minutes (or 35 min. high pressure).

3.   Once the oil is hot, sear the veal for 5 minutes, then deglaze with port wine and brandy. Brown for 2 minutes.

4.   Add shallots, garlic, onions, all mushrooms and sauté for 3 minutes.

5.   Add tomato paste, beans, and beef broth.

6.   Place the lid on the pressure cooker, lock the lid and switch the pressure release valve to CLOSED.

7.   When timer reaches 0, switch the pressure valve to OPEN and remove lid.

8.   Stir in parsley and potato flakes to thicken the gravy.

6

Minutes Under
Pressure

SERVES 6 – 8

Ingredients

For the Pico de Gallo:

3 cups tomato, diced

½ cup red onion, diced

1 clove garlic, chopped

¼ cup fresh cilantro, chopped

3 tbsp. fresh lime juice

2 tbsp. olive oil

Salt and pepper to taste

For the Pasta Dish:

3 tbsp. olive oil

1 lb. ground chicken

½ lb. chorizo sausage, sliced

1 cup onion, diced

1 cup roasted red pepper, diced

1 cup roasted green chili, diced

1 cup corn

1 (15 oz.) can black beans, rinsed
well and drained

2 cups chicken stock

2 tbsp. chipotle in adobo sauce

1 lb. penne pasta

1 tbsp. paprika

2 tsp. cumin

1 tsp. coriander

1 cup sour cream

Baja Chicken Penne

Directions

1.   Combine all Pico de Gallo ingredients in a separate bowl and set aside.

2.   Press the RICE/RISOTTO button and set the time for 6 minutes (6 min. high pressure).

3.   Add oil to the inner pot, and once the oil is hot, brown chicken, chorizo, onions, paprika, cumin and coriander for about 7 minutes.

4.   Add corn, peppers, beans, chipotle, stock and uncooked penne pasta. Stir well.

5.   Lock lid into place and switch the pressure valve to CLOSED.

8.   When timer reaches 0, switch the pressure release valve to OPEN and, once all the pressure has been released, remove lid.

9.   Stir in sour cream and Pico de Gallo.

6

Minutes Under
Pressure

SERVES 6

Ingredients

2 tbsp. olive oil

1½ lbs. elbow macaroni

3½ cups French onion soup

½ Italian baguette, sliced and toasted

½ tsp. onion powder

½ tsp. garlic powder

8 oz. Gruyere cheese (shredded)

8 oz. cheddar cheese (shredded)

1 cup fresh Parmesan grated cheese

½ cup milk

4 oz. sour cream

4 oz. cream cheese

4 oz. mozzarella cheese

Salt and pepper

Whenever you have two foods that are fun and delicious, I never find a problem with twisting them together. I had a lot of fun making this twist on mac and cheese for my son Max who loves both. Or is it a twist on French onion soup? You decide!

Max's French Onion Mac and Cheese

Directions

1.   Place the inner pot in the pressure cooker. Place the oil in the inner pot. Press the RICE/RISOTTO button (or high pressure for 6 minutes).

2.   Add the macaroni and coat with olive oil and sauté for 1 minute.

3.   Add the French onion soup and place the lid on the pressure cooker. Lock the lid and switch the pressure valve to the CLOSED position.

4.   While pasta is cooking, slice your baguette into thin slices. Drizzle with olive oil and sprinkle with onion and garlic powder. Toast in oven until crispy.

5.   Once the timer reaches 0, switch the pressure release valve to OPEN. Once all of the pressure has been released, remove the lid.

6.   Add the milk and all the cheeses except for the mozzarella. Stir well until melted and well incorporated. Place the toasts on the top layer and top with mozzarella. Replace lid, lock lid and press the warm button. Let stand for 5 or 10 minutes until mozzarella is melted.

7.   Salt and pepper to taste.

Eric's Tip: When incorporating the cheese and milk, if it's too thick, feel free to drizzle extra milk in a little bit at a time until you like the consistency.

98

6
Minutes Under Pressure

SERVES 6 – 8

Ingredients

1 lb. box macaroni

4 cups water

2 tsp. salt

½ cup yellow onion, chopped

¾ cup green bell pepper, chopped

1½ tbsp. Old Bay seasoning

1 tsp. ground black pepper

2 tbsp. whole grain mustard

1 lb. crabmeat, preferably back fin or claw

1½ cups milk

2 cups shredded white cheddar cheese

2 cups shredded yellow cheddar cheese

3 oz. softened cream cheese

2 tsp. fresh lemon zest

3 tbsp. fresh parsley, chopped

1 cup seasoned breadcrumbs

This dish brings me back to summers at the shore at the bayside crab shack, only better thanks to the abundance of cheese I added to this recipe.

Maryland Crab Cake Mac and Cheese

Directions

1.   Add water, onion, pepper, salt and macaroni to pot.

2.   Place lid on cooker, lock lid into place, and switch the pressure valve to CLOSED. Press RICE/RISOTTO button (6 min. high pressure).

3.   When timer reaches 0, switch the pressure valve to OPEN and release the steam. Once all the steam has been released, remove lid.

4.   Add milk, cream cheese and stir. Add shredded cheeses slowly and continue to stir.

5.   Add Old Bay, lemon zest, parsley, mustard and black pepper. When all ingredients are incorporated, gently fold in crab and transfer to serving dish. Sprinkle breadcrumbs on top.

7
Minutes Under
Pressure

SERVES 6 – 8

Texas Tommy Mac and Cheese

Ingredients

1 lb. box macaroni

4 cups water

2 tsp. salt

2 tbsp. olive oil

1 cup yellow onion, chopped

1 package hot dogs, cut into ¾ inch pieces

1 fresh jalapeno, seeded and chopped

1½ cups tomato, seeded and diced

2 tbsp. yellow mustard

2 tsp. paprika

2 tsp. cumin

2 tsp. ground black pepper

1½ cups milk

2 cups shredded white cheddar cheese

2 cups shredded Pepper Jack cheese

½ lb. bacon, cooked crispy and chopped

¼ cup scallions chopped

Fresh chopped cilantro for garnish

Directions

1.   Add oil to pot and press the RICE/RISOTTO button and time adjustment button to reach 7 minutes (or 7 min. high pressure).

2.   Once the oil gets hot, add onions, salt and hot dogs. Sauté for 3 minutes or until brown.

3.   Add macaroni and water, and stir.

4.   Place lid on top, lock the lid and switch the pressure valve to CLOSED.

5.   When timer reaches 0, switch the pressure valve to OPEN and, once all the pressure has been released, remove lid.

6.   Add milk, mustard, tomato, jalapeno, black pepper, paprika, cumin and then stir.

7.   Add both chesses slowly while stirring.

8.   Once cheese is melted and ingredients are fully incorporated, transfer to serving dish and garnish with cilantro, crispy bacon and scallions.

5

Minutes Under
Pressure

SERVES 8 – 10

Ingredients

1½ lbs. ground beef

1 (24 oz.) jar of marinara sauce

1 (14.5 oz.) can diced tomatoes

1½ lbs. elbow macaroni

6 cups beef stock

2 tsp. salt

½ tsp. black pepper

1 cup ricotta cheese

1 cup shredded mozzarella
cheese

Clearly, I love mac and cheese, and, being Italian, I love lasagna. Why wait for one or the other when you can eat them at the same time! I had a great time playing around with different flavors for mac and cheese in the pressure cooker. To this day I am still amazed that pasta can be cooked in there. Just the fact that you don't need a strainer or colander makes cooking pasta dishes so much more efficient, not to mention that you will never have a boil over in a pressure cooker like you might in a stockpot.

Mac and Cheese Lasagna

Directions

1. Place inner pot in cooker.

2. Add the ground beef.

3. Hit the BEANS/LENTILS button (or high pressure 5 min).

4. Once the pot is hot, brown the beef until it is no longer pink. Drain fat.

5. Add the marinara, tomatoes, macaroni, stock, salt and pepper. Stir well.

6. Place the lid on the cooker, lock the lid and switch the pressure valve to CLOSED.

7. When the timer reaches 0, switch the pressure valve to OPEN. When steam is completely released, open lid.

8. Stir in ricotta and mozzarella.

Poultry

Poultry is one of my favorite dishes to make in the pressure cooker. In fact my friends will often be surprised at how many times I will order it even out at a fine dining restaurant. The first time I made an entire chicken in the pressure cooker, I actually laughed when I pulled it out of the pot. It simply fell apart, tender and juicy. I still laugh when I make it and try to come up with as many ways as I possibly can to enjoy using the pressure cooker for poultry.

It doesn't matter if you are in the mood for chicken breasts, bone in or filets, frozen or fresh! You can even cook whole chickens with stuffing or thighs and drumsticks; getting great results is so fast and easy in the pressure cooker. Once you get used to cooking under pressure, you will be able to vary some of the times and adapt your very own recipes. As with any meat or poultry, searing the meat before pressure cooking it will yield a more flavorful end result. It is not necessary, but I like the color and flavor it adds, so I don't tend to skip this step.

Ingredients

1 (12 oz.) bag unseasoned cubed stuffing

4 tbsp. butter

1 cup onion, small diced

1 cup celery, small diced

4 cups chicken stock, divided

1 (10.5 oz.) can cream of chicken soup

½ tsp. dried thyme

½ tsp. dried rubbed sage

½ tsp. dried rosemary

½ tbsp. dried parsley

½ tsp. salt

½ tsp. pepper

2 (approx. 4 lb.) whole chickens, giblets removed

1 (2 oz.) box onion soup mix

You can have Sunday dinner any day of the week in just an hour with this wholesome recipe.

Whole Chickens with Herb Stuffing

Directions

1. Place cubed stuffing into a large bowl.

2. Place inner pot in cooker.

3. Add the butter, onion and celery to inner pot.

4. Press the MEAT/CHICKEN button (or brown/sauté mode).

5. Sauté onion and celery for about 5 minutes.

6. Add 2 cups of chicken stock, cream of chicken soup, thyme, sage, rosemary, parsley, salt and pepper.

7. Stir and bring to a boil.

8. Press the cancel/keep warm button (or off/cxl button).

9. Remove inner pot and pour the hot liquid over the cubed stuffing.

10. Place inner pot back into cooker and add the remaining chicken stock. Allow to come to a simmer without the lid.

11. Stir the hot liquid into the stuffing.

12. Let stuffing set for a few minutes, stirring occasionally.

13. When stuffing has absorbed the liquid, spread it out on a baking sheet and let cool.

14. Rub the outside of the chickens with the soup mix and place in the inner pot, legs and cavity facing up and breasts facing the inside.

15. Spoon the stuffing into the cavity of each bird.

16. Place the lid on the cooker, lock the lid and switch the pressure valve to CLOSED.

17. Press the MEAT/CHICKEN button, then press the time adjust button until it reaches 60 minutes (or high pressure 60 min.).

18. When timer reaches 0, press the cancel/keep warm button (or off/cxl button).

19. Let the pressure drop naturally for 10 minutes.

20. Switch the pressure valve to OPEN. When steam is completely released, open lid.

21. Plate and serve.

Eric's Tip: You may have leftover stuffing. That's great! Simply put whatever doesn't fit into a cake pan and bake the extra for leftovers.

15
Minutes Under
Pressure

SERVES 6 – 8

"Toss and Go" Chicken Stew

Ingredients

2 cups chicken stock

½ cup Marsala wine (optional)

2 (10.5 oz.) cans cream of chicken soup

1 tsp. dried thyme

1 tsp. rosemary

1 tsp. minced garlic

2 lbs. boneless skinless chicken breast, diced into ½-inch pieces

2 (1 lb.) bags mixed frozen vegetables

1 (20 oz.) bag refrigerated, diced and partially cooked potatoes

Directions

1.   Place inner pot in cooker. Press the MEAT/CHICKEN button (or high pressure 15 min.).

2.   Add chicken stock, soup, thyme, rosemary, garlic, chicken, vegetables and potatoes and optional Marsala wine.

3.   Stir ingredients together.

4.   Place the lid on the cooker, lock the lid and switch the pressure valve to CLOSED.

5.   When the timer reaches 0, switch the pressure valve to OPEN. When the steam is completely released, open the lid.

6.   Stir and serve.

Eric's Tip: Keeping with the super quick theme, while the stew is cooking, bake some refrigerator biscuits and place the biscuits in the middle of the bowls, and ladle the stew over them.

25
Minutes Under
Pressure

SERVES 6 – 8

Green Garden Chicken Salad

Ingredients

4 each split chicken breasts, bone in and skin on

1 cup water

Salt and pepper

4 cups raw kale, chiffonade

1 cup carrots, shredded

1 cup dried cranberries

1 cup dried apricots, chopped

½ cup red onion, chopped

1 cup celery, chopped

1 clove garlic, chopped

½ cup Italian parsley, chopped

¼ cup fresh basil, chopped

1 cup mayonnaise

¾ cup Greek yogurt

1 tbsp. Dijon mustard

1 tsp. curry powder

Directions

1. Push CHICKEN/MEAT button (or high pressure 25 min).

2. Season chicken generously with salt and pepper.

3. Add water and chicken to the inner pot.

4. Lock the lid and switch the pressure valve to CLOSED.

5. When timer reaches 0, switch the pressure valve to OPEN. Once the steam is released, remove the lid.

6. Cool chicken then chop.

7. Combine all ingredients with cooled chicken and season with salt and pepper.

15
Minutes Under
Pressure

SERVES 4

Ingredients

4 bone-in, skin-on split chicken breasts

3 tbsp. olive oil

1½ cups chicken stock

1 tsp. ground turmeric

1 tsp. ground cumin

½ cup heavy cream

1 tbsp. butter

¼ cup potato flakes

16 oz. fresh baby spinach

Salt and pepper to taste

For the tapenade:

¼ cup roasted pine nuts

¾ cup plump sundried tomatoes

¾ cup pitted kalamata olives

1 small onion, large chopped

¾ cup marinated or grilled mushrooms

1 tsp. fresh garlic

Chicken Breasts with Tomato Tapenade

Directions

1.   Place the inner pot into the pressure cooker. Press the CHICKEN/MEAT button once (or high pressure 15 min).

2.   In a separate bowl, rub salt and pepper and turmeric and cumin onto the chicken.

3.   Add the olive oil to the inner pot and, once the oil is hot, sear all 4 breasts skin side down until they are golden brown. Add chicken stock.

4.   Place the lid on the pressure cooker, lock the lid and switch the pressure valve to CLOSED.

5.   While the chicken is cooking under pressure, make the tapenade by combining all remaining ingredients in a food processor, pulsing until combined but not blended.

6.   Once the pressure cooker timer reaches 0, switch the pressure valve to OPEN. When the steam is completely released, remove the lid.

7.   Set chicken aside and let rest for 5 min. Press the CHICKEN/MEAT button again to get into sauté mode and add cream, butter and potato flakes. Stir and simmer for 3 min. Add fresh spinach and stir gently until it's wilted.

8.   Plate the chicken breasts atop the creamy spinach, and add a generous portion of the tapenade on each breast.

Eric's Tip: This dish is great with couscous.

Optional: Try crumbling some goat cheese around the plate for added flavor.

40
Minutes Under Pressure

SERVES 4 – 6

Ingredients

3 tbsp. olive oil

4½ lbs. chicken legs and thighs (skin on)

1 lb. hot Italian sausage (casing removed to crumble)

½ cup red wine

1 cup celery, chopped

1 cup carrots, chopped

1 cup onions, chopped

2 (28 oz.) cans whole San Marzano tomatoes

2 tbsp. tomato paste

1 jalapeno pepper, diced

½ cup balsamic vinegar

1 tsp. oregano powder

2 tsp. red pepper flakes

1 tsp. dried basil

1 onion powder

2 tbsp. garlic chopped

¼ cup chopped Italian parsley for garnish

Chicken Fra Diablo

Directions

1.   Press the CHICKEN/MEAT button and the cook time selector once (or 40 min. high pressure).

2.   Heat the olive oil and sear the chicken parts until browned.

3.   Remove the chicken and set aside.

4.   Brown and crumble the sausage. Drain excess fat and set meat aside.

5.   Deglaze the pot with red wine then add the remaining ingredients.

6.   Sauté without the lid for 5 minutes.

7.   Add the chicken back into the pot, and stir ingredients.

8.   Place the lid on the pressure cooker, lock the lid and switch the pressure valve to CLOSED.

9.   Once the timer reaches 0, switch the pressure release valve to OPEN. When the steam is completely released, remove the lid.

10. Garnish with fresh Italian parsley and serve.

Eric's Tip: This dish is great when served over any type of rice.

Mustard Glazed Thighs with Wild Rice Pilaf

Ingredients

Glaze:

1/4 cup Dijon mustard

2 tbsp. dark brown sugar

2 tbsp. red wine vinegar

¼ cup ketchup

Chicken and Pilaf:

2 lbs. boneless, skinless chicken thighs, seasoned with salt and pepper

2 tbsp. oil

3 tsp. chopped garlic

1 cup diced onions

1 cup diced carrots

8 oz. sliced mushrooms

2½ cups long grain rice

1½ cups chicken stock

1 tsp. dried thyme

2 tsp. salt

½ tsp. pepper

Directions

1.   In a small bowl, combine the ketchup, brown sugar, vinegar and mustard.

2.   Place inner pot in cooker.

3.   Press the RICE/RISOTTO button (or 6 minutes high pressure).

4.   Add oil and, when the oil is hot, brown chicken.

5.   Remove chicken and place in a bowl and coat with half the mustard glaze.

6.   Add oil, garlic, onions, carrots and mushrooms to inner pot and sauté for 2 minutes.

7.   Add rice, stock, thyme, salt and pepper.

8.   Lay the chicken over surface of rice.

9.   Place the lid on the cooker, lock the lid and switch the pressure valve to CLOSED.

10. When the timer reaches 0, switch the pressure valve to OPEN.

11. When steam is completely released, open lid.

12. Serve with remaining glaze.

Eric's Tip: This makes for a delicious chicken salad recipe the next day; just chop up the leftovers and add some mayonnaise.

30
Minutes Under
Pressure

SERVES 6 – 8

Ingredients

4 lbs. chicken thighs, skin removed

3 tbsp. olive oil

½ cup paprika

1 tsp. salt

1 tbsp. black pepper

½ tsp. ground nutmeg

½ tsp. caraway seed

3 cloves garlic, smashed

1 head Savoy cabbage (can substitute Napa cabbage), cut into 1-inch slices

½ cup chicken broth

½ cup cream cheese

Chicken Paprikash

Directions

1.   Push CHICKEN/MEAT button and time adjustment button to reach 30 minutes (30 min. high pressure). Add olive oil.

2.   Remove skin from chicken thighs. Coat with ¼ c. paprika, salt, pepper and nutmeg.

3.   When the oil is hot, brown the chicken, then remove.

4.   Add half of the cabbage, garlic, onions, caraway and half of remaining paprika. Then place chicken on top of cabbage. Top with remaining cabbage and paprika.

5.   Add chicken broth. Lock the lid and switch the pressure valve to CLOSED.

6.   When timer reaches 0, switch the pressure valve to OPEN. Once the steam is released, remove the lid.

7.   Remove chicken, stir in cream cheese to thicken sauce.

8.   Serve chicken with the sauce.

Ingredients

4 lbs. chicken thighs

3 tbsp. olive oil

1 can unsweetened coconut milk

1 green bell pepper, sliced

1 red bell pepper, sliced

1 yellow bell pepper, sliced

1 medium red onion, sliced

2 cloves garlic chopped

2 tbsp. chopped fresh ginger

1/3 cup fresh cilantro, chopped

3 tbsp. jerk seasoning

1 tsp. salt

1 tsp. paprika

1 tsp. cumin

1 fresh lime, juiced

½ cup potato flakes

Island Chicken

Directions

1.   Push CHICKEN/MEAT button then the time adjustment button to reach 30 minutes (or high pressure 30 min).

2.   Remove skin from chicken thighs. Coat chicken with olive oil, jerk seasoning, paprika, salt and cumin.

3.   When the oil is hot, brown the chicken, then remove.

4.   Add onions, peppers, ginger and garlic. Place chicken on top.

5.   Add coconut milk and place lid on pressure cooker. Lock the lid and switch the pressure valve to CLOSED.

6.   When timer reaches 0, switch the pressure valve to OPEN. Once the steam is released, remove the lid.

7.   Remove chicken, then add potato flakes, cilantro and lime juice. Stir until well incorporated and serve over chicken.

Eric's Tip: Serve over basmati rice, as the aroma of this rice complements the dish.

45

Minutes Under Pressure

SERVES 6 – 8

Ingredients

4 lbs. turkey thighs, skin removed

3 tbsp. olive oil

3 tsp. paprika

3 tsp. cumin

1 (8 oz.) jar prepared mole sauce

2 cups chicken broth

½ cup Mexican chocolate, chopped

Corn tortillas, soft

Queso Fresco, crumbled

Red onion, chopped

Fresh cilantro, chopped

Turkey Mole Street Tacos

Directions

1.   Push CHICKEN/MEAT button and time adjustment button to reach 45 minutes (high pressure 45 min).

2.   Coat turkey thighs with olive oil, paprika and cumin.

3.   When the oil is hot, brown the turkey.

4.   In a separate bowl, combine mole sauce, chicken broth and chocolate. Pour over turkey.

5.   Place the lid on the cooker, lock the lid and switch the pressure valve to CLOSED.

6.   When timer reaches 0, switch the pressure valve to OPEN. Once the steam is released, remove the lid.

7.   Remove turkey and shred meat with two forks then toss in mole sauce.

8.   Serve over warm corn tortillas (two per taco), garnish with queso, red onion and cilantro.

Eric's Tip: Thin-sliced radish and shredded cabbage are traditional street food garnishes that add a refreshing texture and flavor to this dish.

Arroz con Pollo (Chicken with Rice)

Ingredients

3 lbs. chicken thighs,
skin removed

2 tbsp. oil

2 tsp. minced garlic

1 cup onions, medium diced

1 red bell pepper, diced

1 (14.5 oz.) can petite-diced tomatoes

2½ cups uncooked Arborio rice

1 cup frozen peas

1 cup frozen corn

1½ cups chicken stock

2 generous pinches of saffron (or
1 tsp. ground turmeric)

1 tsp. cumin

2 tsp. salt

½ tsp. black pepper

Directions

1.   Place inner pot in cooker.

2.   Press the RICE/RISOTTO button and time adjustment to reach 7 minutes (7 min. high pressure).

3.   Add oil.

4.   Season chicken with salt and pepper

5.   When the oil is hot, brown chicken in two batches.

6.   Remove chicken and set aside.

7.   Add the garlic, onion and pepper, and sauté for 2 minutes.

8.   Add the tomatoes, rice, peas, corn, stock, saffron or turmeric, cumin, salt and pepper.

9.   Stir well, then add chicken.

10. Place the lid on the cooker and switch the pressure valve to CLOSED.

11. When the timer reaches 0, switch the pressure valve to OPEN.

12. When steam is completely released, open the lid.

13. Serve.

15
Minutes Under Pressure

SERVES 4 – 6

Ingredients

6 to 8 skinless chicken thighs

Salt and pepper

3 tbsp. olive oil

½ lb. chorizo sausage, cut into 1-inch slices

½ cup onion, diced

¼ cup celery, diced

¼ cup carrot, diced

½ cup white wine

1 clove garlic, smashed

2 sprigs fresh thyme

3 cups chicken stock

2 cans cannellini beans, rinsed and drained

Chicken Cassoulet

Directions

1.   Place inner pot in cooker and press the CHICKEN/MEAT button (or high pressure 15 min.)

2.   Season chicken with salt and pepper.

3.   Add olive oil to cooker and, when the oil is hot, brown chicken, and then remove chicken and set aside.

4.   Add chorizo and brown 3 to 5 minutes.

5.   Add onion, carrot and celery. Sauté 5 minutes.

6.   Deglaze inner pot with wine.

7.   Add garlic, thyme, stock, beans and chicken.

8.   Place pressure lid on the cooker, lock the lid and switch the pressure valve to CLOSED.

9.   When the timer reaches 0, switch the pressure valve to OPEN. Once all the pressure has been released, remove the lid.

10. Serve.

10 Minutes Under Pressure

SERVES 3 – 6

Ingredients

2 tbsp. olive oil

1 lb. lean ground turkey

3 bell peppers, cut in half length-wise and cleaned of core and seeds

½ cup cooked quinoa

½ cup lentils, rinsed and drained

1 egg white

¾ cup zucchini, grated

¾ cup onion, grated

¾ cup carrot, grated

1 tsp. dried basil

Salt and pepper

1 (15.5 oz.) can tomato sauce

Turkey Quinoa Stuffed Peppers

Directions

1. Place the inner pot into the cooker and press the SOUP/STEW button (or 10 min high pressure).

2. Add oil to the inner pot. When the oil is hot, add the ground turkey and brown it with the lid off.

3. In a separate bowl, combine quinoa, lentils, egg white, zucchini, onion, carrot, basil, salt and pepper. Mix well.

4. When the turkey is cooked through, drain it and discard any leftover fats and oil. Incorporate the turkey into the quinoa mix.

5. Divide the mixture evenly among the halves, stuff them and place the steaming rack into the cooker. Place stuffed peppers on the rack.

6. Pour tomato sauce over the peppers.

7. Place the lid on the pressure cooker, lock the lid and switch the pressure valve to CLOSED.

8. Once the timer reaches 0, switch the pressure valve to OPEN. When the pressure has been fully released, open the lid.

9. Serve.

Eric's Tip: Add some spicy chipotles and cilantro for a delicious Southwestern twist.

Traditionally, you would marinate the chicken in red wine overnight prior to cooking. You can still do that prior to pressure cooking this dish, if you like. I like to think of this as a "Quick" Coq au Vin, and the pressure cooking will infuse the wine flavor into the chicken.

Braised Chicken with Bacon (Coq au Vin)

Ingredients

12 pieces chicken, legs and thighs, skinless

Salt and pepper

¼ cup flour sifted twice

8 strips of thick sliced bacon, sliced into ½" pieces

2 cups frozen pearl onions

¾ lb. crimini mushrooms, sliced

½ cup carrot, diced

½ cup celery, diced

1½ cups red wine (preferably pinot noir)

1 cup chicken stock

1 tbsp. tomato paste

2 cloves garlic, crushed

3 tsp. herbs de provence

1 bay leaf

2 sprigs each, rosemary and thyme (tied with twine for easy removal)

¼ cup potato flakes

¼ cup fresh Italian parsley, chopped

Directions

1.   Season chicken with salt and pepper. Lightly dust with flour, then shake off excess.

2.   Place the bacon into the inner pot. Press the CHICKEN/MEAT button once (or 15 minutes high pressure). When oil is hot, sauté bacon until crispy. Remove to a paper towel to be used as garnish.

3.   Sear chicken in the bacon fat until brown. Remove chicken and set aside.

4.   Add onions, carrot, celery and mushrooms. Sauté in the bacon fat for 5 minutes, then add garlic.

5.   Deglaze pan with red wine.

6.   Add stock, bay leaf, rosemary, thyme, tomato paste, herbs de provence, bacon and chicken.

7.   Place the lid on the pressure cooker, lock the lid and switch the pressure valve to CLOSED.

8.   When the timer reaches 0, switch the pressure release valve to OPEN. When the steam is completely released, remove the lid.

9.   Remove the bay leaf, twined herbs and the chicken. Press the SOUP/STEW button (or brown/sauté mode) once to simmer and thicken the sauce. While simmering, sprinkle in the potato flakes and stir to incorporate. When the sauce is at desired thickness, ladle over the chicken and garnish with crumbled bacon and fresh parsley.

Eric's Tip: This dish is served many ways, but my favorite way is when served over mashed potatoes.

15
Minutes Under Pressure

SERVES 4 – 6

The great thing about kielbasa is that it's already cooked! That means you can bring dinner to the table even faster when you use it. Plus, it's full of flavor and pairs so well with cabbage.

Chicken Cacciatore

Ingredients

6 to 8 pieces skinless chicken legs and thighs

Salt and pepper

1 cup all-purpose flour

3 tbsp. olive oil

1 green pepper, sliced

1 cup yellow onion, sliced

1 oz. dried porcini mushrooms, reconstituted in 1 cup water

2 cloves garlic, smashed

1 tbsp. tomato paste

½ cup red wine

1 (14 ounce) can crushed tomatoes

1 tsp. dried oregano

½ tsp. red chili flakes

1 cup chicken stock

6 leaves fresh basil

Directions

1.   Press the CHICKEN/MEAT button (or 15 minutes high pressure).

2.   Season the chicken with salt and pepper and lightly dredge it in the flour.

3.   Add oil to cooker and, when the oil is hot, brown the chicken. Set chicken aside.

4.   Add pepper and onion to the oil and sauté for 5 minutes. Add mushrooms, garlic and tomato paste.

5.   Deglaze pot with red wine.

6.   Add crushed tomato, oregano, chili flakes, chicken stock and basil.

7.   Place lid on cooker, lock the lid and switch the pressure valve to CLOSED.

8.   When the timer reaches 0, switch the pressure valve to OPEN. Once all the pressure has been released, open the lid.

9.   Serve over your favorite pasta or rice.

10 Minutes Under Pressure

SERVES 6 – 8

Ingredients

3 oz. seasoned rice wine vinegar

½ cup hoisin sauce

2 tbsp. oyster sauce

1½ tsp. sesame oil

3 tsp. sugar

2 lbs. boneless, skinless chicken thighs, cut each thigh into about 6 pcs

2 tbsp. oil

2 tsp. garlic

1 tsp. minced fresh ginger

1 cup medium onion, diced

1 green pepper, diced

1 red pepper, diced

2 stalks celery, diced

2 cups basmati rice

2 cups chicken stock

1½ cups dry roasted cashews

½ cup sliced scallions

Cashew Chicken Rice Bowl

Directions

1. In a bowl, combine the vinegar, hoisin sauce, oyster sauce, sesame oil, and sugar and set aside.

2. Place inner pot in cooker.

3. Press the RICE/RISOTTO button (6 minutes high pressure).

4. Season chicken with salt and pepper.

5. When the oil is hot, in two batches brown chicken pieces.

6. Remove chicken and set aside.

7. Add the garlic, ginger, onion, peppers and celery.

8. Sauté for 2 minutes without the lid.

9. Add the chicken, reserved sauce mixture, rice, and chicken stock.

10. Place the lid on the cooker, lock lid in place and switch the pressure valve to CLOSED.

11. When timer reaches 0, switch the pressure valve to OPEN.

12. When steam is completely released, open lid.

13. Fold in cashews and garnish with scallions.

Eric's Tip: This makes amazing fried rice the next day! Just sauté it and then scramble an egg, then combine.

20
Minutes Under Pressure

SERVES 6 – 8

Chicken Enchilada and Corn Bread Pot Pie

Ingredients

1 cup dry pinto beans

1 tbsp. oil

2 lbs. boneless skinless chicken thighs, large diced and seasoned with salt and pepper

2 tsp. minced garlic

2 cups diced onions

2 green peppers, diced

2 cups frozen corn

2 (10 oz.) cans enchilada sauce

1 cup chicken stock

1 (8.5 oz.) boxed corn muffin mix

1 egg, lightly beaten

3 oz. milk

1 cup shredded cheddar cheese

2 cups shredded Monterey Jack cheese

Sour cream for serving

Directions

1. Place inner pot in cooker.

2. Add beans and cover with an inch of water.

3. Place the lid on the cooker, lock the lid and switch the pressure valve to CLOSED.

4. Press the BEANS/LENTILS button (or high pressure 5 min).

5. When the timer reaches 0, press the cancel/warm button (or off/cxl).

6. Let the pressure in the cooker release naturally without opening pressure valve.

7. When pressure has dropped, remove lid.

8. Drain beans and set aside.

9. Place inner pot in cooker.

10. Add oil.

11. Press SOUP/STEW button then the time adjustment button to reach 15 min. (15 minutes high pressure).

12. When the oil is hot, in 2 batches, brown the diced chicken.

13. Remove chicken, set aside.

14. Add garlic, onions and peppers.

15. Sauté for 3 minutes.

16. Add the chicken, corn, enchilada sauce, and stock. Stir well.

17. In a small bowl combine the corn muffin mix, egg, milk and cheddar cheese.

18. Spoon corn muffin mix over surface of chicken and bean mixture.

19. Top with Monterey Jack cheese.

20. Place the lid on the cooker, lock the lid and switch the pressure valve to CLOSED.

21. When the timer reaches 0, switch the pressure valve to OPEN.

22. When the steam is completely released, open the lid.

23. Serve with sour cream.

Eric's Tip: For a twist on this recipe, substitute canned tomatillos for the enchilada sauce to make it "Verde style."

Pork, Beef and Lamb

If there was a portion of the book that shows off pressure cooking, this is it. Meat benefits from fast cooking under pressure because it's cooked with super heated steam and pressure so it doesn't get dry and comes out moist and juicy.

Although it is optional, I always recommend browning your meat first. The extra flavor is so worth it. When adapting your own recipes, simply make sure there is at least 1-cup total liquid minimum. The less liquid, the more concentrated your broth will be. Use dry spices in the beginning as a very general rule, and I will always add something fresh at the end to add a beautiful color and to brighten up the taste. Experiment with all different chopped herbs; you really can't make a mistake. If you would like a thicker sauce or broth, simply add about a ¼ cup of potato flakes at a time until you reach the desired thickness. To take it up another level add a tablespoon of butter for a nice shine and smooth flavor. The butter at the end is a worthwhile step, and remember that it's a tablespoon for the entire pot. Give it a try even if the recipe doesn't call for it. If all of the ingredients that go into the pot are quality and you use one of these recipes as a general guide for timing, you will be amazed at how forgiving pressure cooking is.

25
Minutes Under Pressure

SERVES 4 – 6

Does your family call this "sauce" or "gravy?" My family calls it gravy due to the presence of meat. Either way, it's delicious!

Italian Pork Ribs and Gravy

Ingredients

2 tbsp. olive oil

2½ lbs. pork ribs

2 tbsp. tomato paste

1 cup water

1 cup red wine

2 tbsp. balsamic vinegar

2 (28 ounce) cans crushed tomatoes

1 large onion, chopped

3 cloves garlic, chopped

2 tsp. dried basil

2 tsp. dried oregano

Directions

1.   Place the inner pot in cooker and add olive oil. Press the CHICKEN/MEAT button (time adjust to reach 25 min high pressure). Heat oil in the bottom of the inner pot.

2.   Brown pork ribs for about 10 minutes. Remove and set aside.

3.   Pour out excess grease and add onion, sautéing for 5 minutes.

4.   Add tomato paste and cook another 2 minutes.

5.   Add garlic and wine, scraping the brown bits off the bottom of the pot and cook for 3 to 5 minutes.

6.   Add water, tomatoes, herbs and ribs.

7.   Place the lid on the cooker, lock the lid and switch the pressure valve to CLOSED.

8.   When the timer reaches zero, switch the pressure valve to OPEN, release the steam and remove the lid.

9.   Season with salt and pepper to taste.

SERVES 6 – 8

Ingredients

4-5 lb. spiral ham, bone in

2 cups quality root beer

½ cup crushed pineapple

¼ cup dark brown sugar

¼ cup cherry jelly

2 tbsp. Dijon mustard

2 tbsp. honey

2 tsp. black pepper

Spiral Ham with Root Beer Glaze

Directions

1. Place steaming rack in bottom of pressure cooker.

2. Add root beer and place ham on top of rack.

3. Push CHICKEN/MEAT button once (or high pressure 15 minutes).

4. Lock the lid and switch the pressure valve to CLOSED.

5. When timer reaches zero, switch the pressure valve to OPEN. Once the steam is released, remove the lid.

6. Remove ham and place on serving platter.

7. Push cancel/keep warm, then press CHICKEN/MEAT button (or brown/sauté mode).

8. Add pineapple, cherry jelly, mustard, honey and black pepper.

9. Simmer without the lid for 5-8 minutes or until thick.

Eric's Tip: This ham is just begging to get tucked into a warm biscuit with jam.

15
Minutes Under
Pressure

**SERVES
ABOUT 8**

Ingredients

3 tbsp. olive oil

3 lbs. hot Italian sausage links

2 (28 oz.) cans San Marzano
peeled tomatoes

2 tbsp. tomato paste

8 bell peppers, sliced

4 onions, sliced

1 cup sweet vermouth

½ cup hot cherry peppers, sliced
(with the juice)

1 tbsp. balsamic vinegar

1 tsp. dried oregano

1 tsp. dried basil

1 tbsp. chopped garlic

Salt and pepper to taste

Serving and Garnish

Pita bread (about 8 rounds,
cut in two)

1 lb. Provolone cheese

Balsamic glaze

Salt and pepper to taste

Where I grew up in NJ, there was a very small takeout place that served the most amazing Italian hot dogs in a pita. I'll never really know what made them so good, but I tried to do something similar with this recipe. Serving it over the pita (as opposed to serving it inside of the pita) makes it easier to eat because I like to put a lot of the sauce on it.

Sausage with Peppers and Onions over Pita

Directions

1.   Place the inner pot in the cooker. Place the oil in the inner pot. Press the CHICKEN/MEAT button (for high pressure 15 min).

2.   Pierce the sausage casings with a fork a few times each. Brown the sausage in the hot oil.

3.   Add all remaining ingredients except serving and garnish. Stir.

4.   Place the lid on the pressure cooker, lock the lid and switch the pressure release valve to CLOSED.

5.   Once the timer reaches 0, the cooker will automatically switch to keep warm. Switch the pressure release valve to OPEN. When the steam is completely released, remove the lid.

6.   Plate the sausage and peppers and some of the sauce overtop pita bread. Top with provolone cheese and drizzle with balsamic glaze.

Eric's Tip: This is also great over crusty Italian bread instead of pita. You will have a copious amount of sauce left over. This sauce is delicious served over pasta for your next meal! It's like two meals in one.

Ingredients

3½ lbs. boneless pork shoulder
(cut in 2 or 3 pieces)

3 tablespoons olive oil

1 cup white onion, chopped

1 cup carrot, chopped

1 cup celery, chopped

3 cloves garlic, smashed

¾ cup white wine

2 cups beef stock

4 tbsp. apple butter

1 cup apple sauce

2 lbs. sauerkraut

2 tsp. fennel seed

1 tsp. oregano powder

Salt and pepper

Braised Pork with Sauerkraut

Directions

1.   Press the CHICKEN/MEAT button and the cook time selector button once (high pressure 40 min).

2.   Heat the olive oil in the inner pot and sear the meat until browned.

3.   Remove the meat and set aside.

4.   Sauté the onion, celery, carrots and garlic for 5 min.

5.   Add remaining ingredients and the meat back into the pot and mix well.

6.   Place the lid on the pressure cooker, lock the lid and switch the valve to CLOSED.

7.   Once the timer reaches 0, switch the pressure release valve to OPEN. When the steam is completely released, remove the lid.

8.   Serve.

Eric's Tip: **Try this dish topped with some fresh finely diced apples for added brightness and texture.**

40

Minutes Under
Pressure

SERVES 4 – 6

Ingredients

4 lbs. boneless country pork ribs

1 tbsp. olive oil

1 pear, peeled and grated

1/3 cup hoisin sauce

¼ cup dark brown sugar

2 tbsp. soy sauce

2 tbsp. fresh ginger, minced

3 tbsp. toasted sesame oil

2 tbsp. chili garlic paste

2 tbsp. rice vinegar

3 tbsp. ketchup

3 cloves garlic, chopped

1 orange, juice and zest
(large peel)

Whole toasted sesame seeds

Chopped scallion

Spicy Korean BBQ Pork

Directions

1.   Push CHICKEN/MEAT button and the cook time selector once
(for 40 min high pressure).

2.   In a separate bowl, combine pear, hoisin, soy sauce, ginger, toasted
sesame oil, chili garlic paste, rice vinegar, ketchup, garlic and orange
juice and zest.

3.   Add oil to the inner pot, and when the oil is hot, brown the pork.
Then add the sauce mixture.

4.   Lock the lid and switch the pressure valve to CLOSED.

5.   When timer reaches 0, switch the pressure valve to OPEN. Once
the steam is released, remove the lid.

6.   Remove pork, garnish with sesame seeds and scallion.

Eric's Tip: **This makes awesome lettuce wraps garnished
with fresh pickled vegetables and crispy fried rice noodles.**

French Country Pork Loin

Ingredients

4 lbs. pork loin, bone-in

3 tbsp. olive oil

1 cup carrots, rustic cut

1 cup parsnips, rustic cut

1 cup celery, rustic cut

1 cup bliss potatoes

1 each medium onion, rustic cut

2 clove garlic, smashed

1 cup beef stock

1 cup apple sauce

3 tbsp. Dijon mustard

3 tsp. herbs de province

¼ cup potato flakes (optional)

2 tsp. salt

Pepper to taste

Directions

1. Season pork with salt and pepper.

2. Press CHICKEN/MEAT button, then press cook time selector twice to set for 60 min. (or 60 min. high pressure).

3. Add oil to the pot. When the oil is hot, sear the pork.

4. Add vegetables, garlic and herbs.

5. Combine stock, applesauce and Dijon. Pour over vegetables.

6. Place lid on cooker, lock the lid and switch the pressure valve to CLOSED.

7. Once the timer reaches 0, switch the pressure release valve to OPEN. Once the pressure has been released, open the lid.

8. Serve.

Eric's Tip: You can add ⅓ cup of brandy or cognac to give it a little punch.

Note: Herbs de Province consists of dried savory, marjoram, rosemary, thyme, oregano and sometimes lavender. It can be found as a blend at your market, but if you can't find it, just combine in equal parts the dried herbs I've listed.

25
Minutes Under
Pressure

SERVES 6 – 8

Chorizo Grits

Ingredients

3 tbsp. olive oil

2 cups yellow corn grits

3 cups chicken stock

3 cups water

1 lb. chorizo sausage, chopped

1 cup onion, small chopped

2 tsp. salt

2 cups shredded cheddar cheese

½ cup scallions, chopped

Directions

1.   Push RICE/RISOTTO button and hit time adjustment button to reach 25 minutes (25 min. high pressure).

2.   Heat oil. Sauté onions, salt and chorizo for 5 minutes.

3.   Add grits, chicken stock and water.

4.   Place the lid on the cooker, lock the lid and switch the pressure valve to CLOSED.

5.   When timer reaches 0, switch the pressure valve to OPEN. Once all the pressure has been released, remove the lid.

6.   Stir in cheese and scallions.

Eric's Tip: To make a great base for eggs any style, pour the grits into a loaf pan and let cool. Then slice and sauté until crispy! Place the eggs on top and enjoy breakfast.

SERVES 6 – 8

Ingredients

2 racks of pork ribs, cut into thirds

1 cup dark brown sugar

3 tbsp. paprika

2 tbsp. cumin

¼ cup ground espresso

1 tbsp. salt

2 tbsp. black pepper

1 tbsp. garlic powder

1 (16 oz.) jar guava jelly

¼ cup hot water

Café Cubano Ribs

Directions

1. Push CHICKEN/MEAT button and the cook time selector until you reach 45 min. (45 min high pressure).

2. Combine brown sugar with espresso and spices then rub on ribs. Set aside.

3. Heat guava jelly and water in microwave for 30 seconds to loosen it up.

4. Place ribs standing on end inside pressure cooker.

5. Pour guava jelly over ribs. Lock the lid and switch the pressure valve to CLOSED.

6. When timer reaches 0, switch the pressure valve to OPEN. Once the steam is released, remove the lid.

7. Remove ribs, reduce sauce to desired consistency and pour over ribs.

Szechuan Dry Spiced Ribs with Miso Glaze

Ingredients

2 racks of pork ribs
(St. Louis style or baby back),
cut into thirds

Dry Rub

3 tbsp. Szechuan peppercorns

3 each star anise

1 tsp. fennel seed

1 tsp. whole coriander seed

3 each whole cloves

1 tsp. whole black pepper

1 tsp. ground ginger

1 tsp. Chinese 5 spice powder

1 tsp. kosher salt

Miso Glaze

½ cup white miso

3 tbsp. brown sugar

2 tbsp. toasted sesame oil

3 tbsp. sake

1 tbsp. rice vinegar

2 tbsp. soy sauce

2 tbsp. hoisin

Directions

1.   Push CHICKEN/MEAT button and time adjustment to reach 45 min. (or high pressure 45 min).

2.   In a dry sauté pan over medium heat, toast Szechuan pepper corns, star anise, coriander seed, clove and black pepper until fragrant. Let cool and place in a coffee/spice grinder or use mortar and pestle. Add ground ginger, 5-spice and salt. Grind until fine.

3.   Coat ribs with dry rub and let sit for 30 minutes.

4.   Place ribs standing upright inside pressure cooker. Add 1 cup of water, lock the lid and switch the pressure valve to CLOSED.

5.   While ribs are cooking, in a bowl whisk together all of the miso glaze ingredients.

6.   When timer reaches 0, switch the pressure valve to OPEN. Once the steam is released, remove the lid.

7.   Remove ribs and place on baking tray. Brush with miso glaze and place under broiler until nice and brown.

45

Minutes Under Pressure

SERVES 6 – 8

Ingredients

3 tbsp. olive oil

1 medium onion, sliced

1 tbsp. tomato paste

1 tbsp. apple cider vinegar

1 tsp. brown sugar

1 clove garlic, chopped

1 tbsp. fresh ground black pepper

1 tsp. kosher salt

1 cup beef broth

2 lbs. collard greens, washed with stems removed

4 smoked ham hocks

Southern Collard Greens with Ham Hocks

Directions

1.   Place the inner pot in cooker and push CHICKEN/MEAT button and the time adjustment button to reach 45 min. (high pressure 45 min).

2.   Slice collards in 1-inch strips.

3.   Heat olive oil in inner pot, and then add onion and garlic. Sauté onion and garlic for 2 minutes. Add remaining ingredients except collard greens and the ham hocks. Stir, then sauté for one more minute.

4.   Add collard greens and stir to coat.

5.   Add ham hocks and place lid on pressure cooker. Lock the lid and switch the pressure valve to CLOSED.

6.   When timer reaches 0, switch the pressure valve to OPEN. Once the steam is released, remove the lid.

7.   Remove ham hocks and let cool to touch. Pick meat off hocks and chop then add back into collards.

Eric's Tip: Makes a great side dish to fried chicken and cornbread.

Note: The best way to clean collard greens is to put them in your clean, empty sink, then fill up your sink with water. Use your hands to agitate the collard greens as the sink is filling up. Let them sit for 5 minutes. Agitate some more, and then lift the collard greens out while water is running over them. Place on towels or in a colander.

30
Minutes Under Pressure

SERVES 8 – 10

Ingredients

Loaves:

3 lbs. mixed ground pork, ground veal and ground beef

1½ cups onion, small chopped

2 small cloves of garlic, minced

3 egg yolks, lightly beaten

1 cup tomato ketchup

2 tbsp. A1-steak sauce

1 cup dried or Panko breadcrumbs

2 tsp. onion powder

Salt and pepper, to taste

½ cup chopped fresh parsley, plus more for garnish

Sauce:

4 oz. soy sauce

1 oz. rice vinegar

3 tbsp. orange juice frozen concentrate

4 oz. ketchup

1 tbsp. minced garlic

2 oz. maple syrup

1 (28 oz.) can whole, peeled tomatoes, drained

¼ cup potato flakes

Ok, this is really my mom's recipe, but I did make a few changes to make it my own. Making meatloaf in the pressure cooker yields a very tender and juicy result. I like playing around with flavors in this classic American dinner.

ET's Sweet and Savory Meatloaf

Directions

1.   Combine loaf ingredients in a large bowl, mixing well.

2.   Divide into 2 equal loaves so that they fit without stacking. Think ovals placed on their sides.

3.   Combine the sauce ingredients except tomatoes in a separate bowl.

4.   Place the loaves in pressure cooker and press the MEAT/CHICKEN button once then the time adjustment button until the timer reads 30 minutes (or 30 min. high pressure). Pour the sauce over the loaves and then pour the tomatoes over the top.

5.   Put the lid on the pressure cooker, lock the lid and switch the pressure release valve to the CLOSED position.

6.   Once the timer reaches 0, switch the pressure release valve to OPEN. Once all of the steam has been released, open the lid.

7.   Remove the loaves using a spatula and tongs and place on a platter and let rest for 5 minutes.

8.   In the inner pot, sprinkle potato flakes into the sauce to thicken it.

9.   Ladle the pressure cooker sauce over the meatloaves, and garnish with fresh parsley. Serve.

Eric's Tip: The sauce in this recipe is really my "anytime sauce" because I use it often on ribs, chicken, pork chops, etc. It tastes great with just about anything!

**SERVES
ABOUT 8**

Ingredients

3 tbsp. olive oil

3-3 1/2 lbs. beef brisket (cut into 4-6 pieces)

2 cups leeks, cleaned and sliced thin

2 cups carrots, sliced

½ cup dry red wine

2 cups. red bliss potatoes, large chopped

1 tsp. thyme

2 tsp. Worcester sauce

½ tsp. ground ginger

1 tbsp. red wine vinegar

3 oz. orange liqueur

¼ cup frozen orange concentrate

1½ cups beef stock

2 tomatoes, chopped large

1 tbsp. minced garlic

1 tbsp. coarse black pepper

1 tbsp. butter

¼ cup heavy cream

¼ cup potato flakes

1 orange segmented with zest reserved for garnish

Brisket is my absolute favorite cut of beef for the pressure cooker. I love how it shreds and picks up flavor so well. This is a play on a dish my old roommate's mom used to make. The flavor of the oranges really brightens it up.

Beef Brisket with Leeks and Orange

Directions

1.   Place the inner pot into the pressure cooker and press the CHICKEN/MEAT button once and the cook time selector twice (60 min. high pressure).

2.   Add the olive oil to the inner pot, and, once the oil is hot, sear the beef brisket pieces until browned.

3.   Add the leeks, carrots and wine and sauté until the leeks soften.

4.   Add all remaining ingredients except for the cream, butter and zest and stir to incorporate.

5.   Place the lid on the pressure cooker, lock the lid and switch the pressure release valve to CLOSED.

6.   Once the timer reaches 0, switch the pressure release valve to OPEN. When all of the steam has been released, open the lid.

7.   Remove the meat and set aside.

8.   Add the butter and heavy cream to the inner pot and stir well. Sprinkle the potato flakes in to thicken the sauce.

9.   Slice the brisket and ladle the sauce over the meat. Sprinkle some orange zest on top and serve with orange segments as garnish.

40
Minutes Under Pressure

SERVES 4 – 6

Ingredients

3½ lbs. beef short ribs

Salt and pepper

2 tbsp. Chinese 5 spice powder

2 tbsp. sesame oil

2 tbsp. olive oil

¾ cup sherry wine

1½ cups beef stock

½ cup orange marmalade

1 clove garlic

¾ cup hoisin sauce

1 tbsp. fresh ginger, minced

2 scallions, chopped

1 tbsp. toasted sesame seeds

¼ cup fresh cilantro, chopped

Chinese 5 Spice Short Ribs

Directions

1.   Season ribs with salt, pepper and 5 spice powder.

2.   Pour the olive and sesame oil into the inner pot and press the CHICKEN/MEAT button then the cook time selector once to reach 40 min. (40 min. high pressure).

3.   Once the oil is hot, place the ribs into the inner pot until nicely browned. Set ribs aside.

4.   Degrease inner pot, and add sherry to deglaze pot.

5.   Add stock, marmalade, garlic, ginger and hoisin. Mix well.

6.   Add ribs back into pot. Place lid on the pressure cooker, lock the lid and switch the pressure valve to CLOSED.

7.   When the timer reaches 0, switch the pressure valve to OPEN. When the steam is completely released, remove the lid.

8.   Plate and garnish with scallion, sesame seeds and cilantro.

Eric's Tip: **To make this a more complete meal, serve over fluffy rice or lo mein noodles.**

SERVES 6 – 8

BBQ Pot Roast

Ingredients

2 tbsp. olive oil

3-3 ½ lbs. of chuck roast

½ tsp. each salt and pepper

1 cups wild mushrooms, sliced

1 cups carrots, large chopped

1 ½ cups onions, chopped

1 cup celery, chopped

1 ½ cups large chopped potatoes

2 cups beef stock

1 cup BBQ sauce

¼ cup orange marmalade

1 tbsp. apple cider vinegar

¼ cup tomato paste

½ cup dry red wine

2 tbsp. garlic, finely chopped

½ tsp. cumin

1 tsp. thyme

½ tsp. rosemary

½ tsp. mustard powder

½ tsp. coarse ground pepper

¼ cup chopped parsley (optional)

1 tbsp. butter

½ cup instant potato flakes

Salt and pepper to taste

Directions

1. Place olive oil in inner pot.

2. Press the CHICKEN/MEAT button once and then the cook time selector twice for 60 minutes (60 minutes high pressure).

3. Salt and pepper the meat and place it into the hot oil to sear. Sear all sides for a few minutes until nicely browned. Set the meat aside.

4. Sauté the vegetables for 5 minutes, then add the meat back in.

5. Add the remaining ingredients except butter and potato flakes.

6. Place the lid on the pressure cooker. Lock the lid and switch the pressure valve to the CLOSED position.

7. Once the timer reaches 0, switch the pressure release valve to the OPEN position. When all of the steam is released, open the lid.

8. Take the meat out and let it "rest." Hit the CHICKEN/MEAT button once again and simmer the sauce that remains in the pot for 10 minutes on high heat.

9. Add the butter and potato flakes and stir to thicken and incorporate.

10. Slice the meat and ladle sauce overtop to serve.

Eric's Tip: Using brisket instead of chuck roast puts a whole new twist on this recipe.

35 Minutes Under Pressure

SERVES 4 – 6

Ingredients

8 top-round beef cutlets, pounded flat

3 tbsp. olive oil

Salt and pepper for seasoning

2 heads of fennel, sliced

1 medium onion, sliced

1 (28 oz.) can of whole peeled tomatoes

3 cloves garlic, smashed

4 slices mozzarella

2 oz. prosciutto

3 oz. Pancetta

3 oz. cappicola

3 oz. Genoa Salami

3 oz. soppressata

½ cup seasoned breadcrumbs

¼ cup fresh basil, chopped

½ cup grated Parmesan cheese

½ tsp. crushed red pepper

This has just a bit of pre-work before you can pressure cook it, but you have to trust me that it's worth it. We used to beg our grandmother to make this for us when we went to see her on Sundays. She never let us down. She stuffed hers with spinach, pine nuts and raisins. Simply put, this is beef that is filled and then rolled. Classically, it's called "Involtini," but in North Jersey we always referred to it as "Braciole." I put some fun and flavorful alternatives to this in the book and I hope you will try each one. Serve it alone or over pasta or rice.

Beef Braciole Siciliano

Directions

1.   Push CHICKEN/MEAT button then the time adjustment button to reach 35 min. (high pressure 35 min).

2.   In a separate bowl, combine breadcrumbs, basil, parmesan and red pepper.

3.   Overlap two cutlets side by side. Lay mozzarella, prosciutto, cappicola, soppressata and salami on top of beef, sprinkling breadcrumb mixture between layers. Roll tightly and secure with toothpicks.

4.   Pour oil into the hot inner pot and sear meat rolls. Remove and set aside.

5.   Add fennel, onion, garlic, and tomatoes. Stir and sauté for 2 minutes. Place rolls back in cooker.

6.   Lock the lid and switch the pressure valve to CLOSED.

7.   When timer reaches zero, do not open the valve. Instead, allow the steam to release naturally. Once the steam has been released, remove the lid.

Eric's Tip: Enjoy with fava beans and a nice Chianti.

153

SERVES 4 – 6

Beef Braciole Florentine

Ingredients

1 (16 oz.) bag frozen cut spinach, thawed and squeezed dry

½ cup pine nuts, toasted

¾ cup shredded Pecorino Romano cheese

2/3 cup golden raisins, divided

Salt and pepper for seasoning

8 top-round beef cutlets, pounded flat

3 tbsp. olive oil

2 heads of fennel, sliced

1 medium onion, sliced

1 (28 oz.) can of crushed tomatoes

3 cloves garlic, smashed

Directions

1.   Push CHICKEN/MEAT button and time adjustment button to reach 25 minutes (or high pressure 25 min).

2.   In a separate bowl, combine spinach, pine nuts, Pecorino, and ⅓ cup of the raisins. Season with salt and pepper.

3.   Overlap two cutlets side by side. Spread ¼ of spinach mixture per roll.

4.   Roll tightly and secure with toothpicks. Season with salt and pepper.

5.   Heat oil in the inner pot, and sear the meat rolls. Remove and set aside.

6.   Add fennel, onion, garlic, tomatoes and other half of raisins and sauté for 3 minutes. Place the meat rolls back into the cooker.

7.   Lock the lid and switch the pressure valve to CLOSED.

8.   When timer reaches 0, do not open the valve. Instead, allow the steam to release naturally. Once the steam has been released, remove the lid.

8.   Serve.

Beef Braciole
Pane con Uovo

Ingredients

3 cups stale bread cubes

1 cup milk

3 eggs, hard boiled and chopped

½ cup grated Parmesan cheese

½ cup sundried tomatoes in olive oil, chopped

¼ cup fresh basil, chopped

Salt and pepper for seasoning

8 top-round beef cutlets, pounded flat

3 tbsp. olive oil

2 heads of fennel, sliced

1 medium onion, sliced

3 cloves garlic, smashed

1 (28 oz.) can of crushed tomatoes

Directions

1. Push MEAT/CHICKEN button and time adjustment button to reach 25 minutes (or high pressure 25 min).

2. Soak bread in milk until it softens, then squeeze out extra milk. Combine with eggs, Parmesan, sundried tomatoes and basil. Season with salt and pepper.

3. Overlap two cutlets side by side. Spread ¼ of bread mixture per roll.

4. Roll tightly and secure with toothpicks. Season with salt and pepper.

5. Heat oil in inner pot and sear the meat rolls. Remove and set aside.

6. Add fennel, onion, garlic, and tomatoes and sauté for 3 minutes. Place the meat rolls back in cooker.

7. Lock the lid and switch the pressure valve to CLOSED.

8. When timer reaches 0, do not open the valve. Instead, allow the steam to release naturally. Once the steam has been released, remove the lid.

9. Serve.

25
Minutes Under
Pressure

SERVES 4 – 6

Ingredients

8 top-round beef cutlets, pounded flat

Salt and pepper for seasoning

3 cups broccoli rabe, blanched and chopped

½ cup roast red peppers, julienned

4 oz. sharp provolone, sliced

3 tbsp. olive oil

2 heads of fennel, sliced

1 medium onion, sliced

1 (28 oz.) can of crushed tomatoes

3 cloves garlic, smashed

Beef Braciole South Philly Style

Directions

1.   Push MEAT/CHICKEN button and the time adjustment button to reach 25 minutes (or high pressure 25 min).

2.   Overlap two cutlets side by side. Layer broccoli rabe, provolone and roasted peppers on beef.

3.   Roll tightly and secure with toothpicks. Season with salt and pepper.

4.   Heat oil in the inner pot and sear the meat rolls. Remove and set aside.

5.   Add fennel, onion, garlic, and tomatoes ands sauté for 3 minutes. Place rolls back in cooker.

6.   Lock the lid and switch the pressure valve to CLOSED.

7.   When timer reaches 0, do not open the valve. Instead, allow the steam to release naturally. Once the steam has been released, remove the lid.

8.   Serve.

Eric's Tip: Make this an awesome sub by tucking the braciole into a roll!

45

Minutes Under
Pressure

MAKES APPROX.
10 ROLLS

Ingredients

1 large head of savoy cabbage

3 tbsp. olive oil

2 lbs. ground beef

¾ cup long grain rice, cooked and cooled

½ cup yellow onion, small chopped

½ cup green pepper, small chopped

½ cup portabella mushroom, small chopped

2 cloves garlic small chopped

1 tbsp. Worcestershire sauce

2 tsp. kosher salt

2 tsp. ground black pepper

2 tsp. fresh thyme, chopped

1 (28 oz.) can of chopped tomatoes

½ cup red wine vinegar

¼ cup brown sugar

¼ cup dried figs, chopped

½ cup beef broth

Stuffed Cabbage

Directions

1.   Remove the core from cabbage and gently peel off leaves keeping them in one piece.

2.   Bring a pot of salted water to a boil. Blanch cabbage for 2-4 min. or until tender, and then place into ice water to cool.

3.   Pat leaves dry, then cut out the thick part of the rib. Set aside.

4.   In a large mixing bowl, mix beef, rice, onion, pepper, mushroom, garlic, salt, pepper, thyme and Worcestershire.

5.   Lay a cabbage leaf flat and place a ½ cup of beef mixture formed into a small oval at the cut end. Roll forward tucking the sides in as you go.

6.   Coat bottom of the inner pot with olive oil, gently place rolls in alternating layers making sure to leave a little space in between them.

7.   Add tomatoes, vinegar, brown sugar, figs and broth.

8.   Lock lid into place and press CHICKEN/MEAT button, then hit the time adjust button to reach 45 minutes (45 minutes high pressure).

9.   When timer reaches zero, switch the pressure valve to OPEN. Once all of the pressure has been released, remove the lid.

10. Gently remove rolls from cooker and place on dish.

11. Press CHICKEN/MEAT button (or brown/sauté mode) and continue to reduce sauce until thickened.

60
Minutes Under Pressure

SERVES 6 – 8

Ingredients

6 strips of bacon, chopped

3½ lbs. beef stewing cubes

1/3 cup flour

1½ cups pearl onions, peeled

3 cloves garlic, smashed

1 lb. carrots, peeled and cut in 1-inch pieces

4 ribs celery, cut in 1-inch pieces

1lb. crimini mushrooms

½ cup brandy

3 tbsp. tomato paste

2 cups beef stock

2½ cups red wine

4 sprigs fresh thyme

2 bay leaves

½ cup potato flakes

Salt and Pepper to taste

Beef Bourguignon

Directions

1.   Press the CHICKEN/MEAT button once and press the cook time selector button twice until you reach 60 minutes (60 min. high pressure).

2.   Place the chopped bacon in the inner pot and sauté until crispy, remove and set aside.

3.   Season beef cubes with salt and pepper, and dust with flour. Add the stew cubes and sear until all sides are browned, remove and set aside.

4.   Add the onions, garlic, carrots, celery, and mushrooms. Sauté for 5 minutes. Add the brandy and sauté for another 2 minutes. Stir in tomato paste.

5.   Add the beef, bacon, beef stock, red wine and thyme.

6.   Put the lid on the pressure cooker, lock the lid and switch the pressure release valve to the CLOSED position.

7.   Once the timer reaches 0, switch the pressure release valve to OPEN. Once all of the steam has been released, open the lid.

8.   Sprinkle in the potato flakes to thicken the sauce.

9.   Season with salt and pepper.

10. Serve over egg noodles.

60
Minutes Under Pressure

SERVES 2 – 4

Ingredients

3 tbsp. olive oil

1 (4 lb.) rack of pork spare ribs, cut in 2-rib pieces

1 green pepper, cut into strips

1 large onion, sliced

2 cloves garlic

½ cup red wine

1 tsp. Italian seasoning

1 tsp. red chili flakes

¼ cup fresh basil, chopped

Salt and pepper to taste

Sicilian Ribs

Directions

1.   Press the CHICKEN/MEAT button once and press the Cook Time Selector button twice until you reach 60 minutes (60 min. high pressure).

2.   Season ribs with salt and pepper. Place ribs in inner pot and sear on all sides until browned. Remove and set aside

3.   Add the onions, peppers, and garlic. Sauté for 5 minutes. Add the red wine and deglaze pot.

4.   Add the tomatoes, Italian seasoning and red chili flakes. Stir to combine.

5.   Add the ribs, submerging into the sauce.

6.   Put the lid on the pressure cooker, lock the lid and switch the pressure release valve to the CLOSED position.

7.   Once the timer reaches 0, switch the pressure release valve to OPEN. Once all of the steam has been released, open the lid.

8.   Remove ribs, cover and let them rest. Add tomato paste to thicken sauce. Season to taste with salt and pepper.

9.   Plate ribs and serve with some sauce poured over top. Sprinkle with fresh basil. Serve.

**MAKES ABOUT
6 CUPS**

Ingredients

2 tbsp. olive oil

½ cup diced pancetta or speck

1 lb. beef stewing cubes,
¼ inch diced

1 lb. ground meatloaf mix

1 cup chopped onion

½ chopped carrot

½ cup chopped celery

2 cloves garlic chopped

1 (28 oz.) can crushed tomatoes

1 cup red wine

1 cup milk

1 tbsp. ground pepper

1 tsp. cinnamon

1 tbsp. butter

2 bay leaves

Freshly grated Parmesan cheese

Rustic Bolognese Sauce

Directions

1.   Place oil into the inner pot and push the SOUP/STEW button once and the time adjustment button once to reach 30 minutes (30 min. high pressure).

2.   Add pancetta and render the fat until crispy, then remove and set aside.

3.   Add beef cubes and brown for 5 minutes, and then remove and set aside.

4.   Add ground pork and brown 5 minutes, then remove and set aside.

5.   Reduce heat and add onions, carrot, celery and wine and sweat for 5 minutes.

6.   Add beef, pork, pancetta, and all remaining ingredients and stir until well incorporated.

7.   Put the lid on the cooker, lock the lid and switch the pressure valve to CLOSED.

8.   Once the timer and counted down to zero, switch the pressure release valve to OPEN. Once the pressure is released, open the lid.

9.   Remove bay leaves.

10. Serve over your favorite pasta and garnish with Parmesan cheese.

20
Minutes Under Pressure

SERVES 6 – 8

Old World Meatballs and Rice

Ingredients

Mixture for meatballs:

3 lbs. ground beef

1 cup bread crumbs

1 cup cooked rice (cooled)

1 tsp. salt

1 tsp. pepper

2 cloves garlic, minced

2 tsp. onion powder

3 eggs

¼ cup parsley, chopped

Additional ingredients:

2 cups additional cooked rice

3 tbsp. olive oil

1 tsp. fennel seeds

½ tsp. mustard powder

3-10.5 oz. cans condensed tomato soup

2 cups chicken stock

1 medium head cabbage, cut into 16ths

Directions

1.   Make the meatballs. Set aside.

2.   Place the inner pot in the cooker. Press the CHICKEN/MEAT button and hit the time adjustment button to reach 20 min. (20 min high pressure). Add olive oil and allow it to heat up for about a minute, then add meatballs. Add all the additional ingredients to the inner pot.

3.   Place the lid on the cooker, lock the lid and switch the pressure release valve to CLOSED.

4.   Once the timer reaches zero, the cooker will automatically switch to KEEP WARM. Switch the pressure release valve to OPEN. When the steam is completely released, remove the lid.

5.   Serve.

Eric's Tip: For a variation on this recipe, substitute ground sausage for the ground beef and stir in pesto sauce at the end.

SERVES 8 – 10

Ingredients

4-6 lbs. flank steak

3 tbsp. olive oil

1 medium onion, sliced

3 cloves garlic, chopped

1 tbsp. paprika

1 tbsp. cumin

1 tsp. ground coriander

2 tsp. kosher salt

1 tsp. fresh ground black pepper

4 oz. can of chopped green chilies

14 oz. can crushed tomato

2 tbsp. Worcestershire

Ropa Vieja

Directions

1. Slice flank steak in thirds across the grain.

2. Toss with dry spices, onions, garlic and Worcestershire. Wrap and refrigerate for 30 minutes.

3. Push CHICKEN/MEAT button then the time adjustment button to reach 55 minutes (or high pressure 55 min).

4. Place the inner pot into cooker and heat oil, then sear the flank steak.

5. Add chilies and tomato. Lock the lid and switch the pressure valve to CLOSED.

6. When timer reaches zero, switch the pressure valve to OPEN. Once the steam is released, remove the lid.

7. Remove steak and shred with 2 forks. Toss with sauce.

Eric's Tip: Serve over Cuban rice and beans.

60 Minutes Under Pressure

SERVES 6 – 8

Ingredients

4 lbs. boneless chuck roast

3 tbsp. olive oil

1 medium onion, sliced

1 cup golden raisins

1 (28 oz.) can crushed tomatoes

½ cup red wine

½ cup cider vinegar

3 cloves garlic, chopped

1 tsp. caraway seed

½ tsp. dried dill

1 cup ginger snap cookie crumbs

I was very lucky to come from Italian and German descent. Both of my grandmothers were great cooks, and yet they couldn't have been more different in their looks, mannerisms, and recipe file. Of course what they did have in common was that they never wrote a recipe down! If you asked them how they made a dish, they never seemed to give you the entire story. It wasn't until much later we found out when my grandmother referred to a cup of something, she was referring to her large coffee cup! No wonder nothing we tried ever turned out the right way. Anyway, this was one of Grandma Theiss's specialties. I tried to figure out a way to make it quickly and easily in the pressure cooker. One day I'll figure out her actual recipe, but until then…

Sauerbraten

Directions

1.   Push CHICKEN/MEAT button three times to reach 60 minutes (high pressure 60 min).

2.   Heat olive oil then brown the beef.

3.   Add onions, raisins, crushed tomato, red wine, cider vinegar, garlic, caraway seed and dried dill.

4.   Place lid on pressure cooker. Lock the lid and switch the pressure valve to CLOSED.

5.   When timer reaches zero, switch the pressure valve to OPEN. Once the steam is released, remove the lid.

6.   Remove beef, then stir in ginger snap crumbs.

7.   Pour the sauce over the beef and serve.

Eric's Tip: Serve this atop crusty bread and add a little crumbled bleu cheese for the best open-faced roast beef sandwich.

Smoked Beef Brisket

Ingredients

1 (3 lb.) beef brisket or pot roast

1 tbsp. olive oil

2 tbsp. honey

1 large bottle of your favorite BBQ sauce

3 cloves garlic, crushed

1 onion, minced

Salt and pepper

½ tbsp. liquid smoke

1½ cups red wine

½ cup water

Directions

1.   Place the inner pot in cooker and hit the CHICKEN/MEAT button then the time adjustment button to reach 45 minutes (or 45 min. high pressure).

2.   Add olive oil to bottom of inner pot and brown beef on all sides.

3.   Remove beef and drain oil. Return beef to inner pot.

4.   Top beef with honey and lightly rub into top of beef.

5.   Add remaining ingredients.

6.   Place lid on cooker, lock the lid and switch the pressure valve to CLOSED.

7.   Once the timer reaches zero, switch the pressure valve to OPEN. Release steam, then remove the lid and serve brisket with broth.

Eric's Tip: For an extra tasty taco, place slices of the brisket on a flour tortilla, add sauce, top with cheese, guacamole, diced tomatoes and lettuce.

40

Minutes Under
Pressure

SERVES 4 – 6

Ingredients

3½ lbs. beef short ribs

Salt and pepper

½ cup flour

4 tbsp. olive oil

1 yellow onion, chopped

½ cup celery, diced

½ cup carrot, diced

2 cloves garlic, smashed

6 oz. tomato paste

2 cups red wine

1 qt. beef stock

2 bay leaves

1 tbsp. orange zest

1 tbsp. lemon zest

Fresh Italian parsley, chopped

My wife loves this dish so much that we served it at our wedding. Again, it's just a fancy name for braised meat, sort of an Italian pot roast. I used short ribs here but it's great with the classic veal shanks. If you don't like veal, you can try it with lamb or pork shanks.

Short Rib Osso Bucco

Directions

1.   Season ribs with salt and pepper and dust with flour.

2.   Pour the olive oil into the inner pot and press the SOUP/STEW button and the time adjustment button to reach 40 minutes (40 min. high pressure).

3.   Place ribs into the inner pot in a single layer until nicely browned. You will need to do this in 2 batches.

4.   Set ribs aside.

5.   Add onions, celery and carrots to inner pot and sauté for one minute.

6.   Add red wine to the inner pot and deglaze, then add garlic, tomato paste, beef stock and bay leaves.

7.   Add ribs back into the pot. Place lid on the pressure cooker, lock the lid, and switch the pressure valve to CLOSED.

8.   Once the timer reaches 0, switch the pressure release valve to OPEN. When the steam is completely released, remove the lid.

9.   Plate and garnish with Italian parsley, orange and lemon zest.

SERVES 6 – 8

Lamb Vindaloo

Ingredients

1 tbsp. turmeric

1 tbsp. ground coriander

2 tsp. ground cumin

2 tbsp. paprika

1 tsp. dry mustard

1 tsp. cayenne pepper

¼ tsp. ground cardamom

½ tsp. cinnamon

2 tsp. kosher salt

4 lbs. lamb stew meat, 2-inch cubes

1 medium onion, sliced

3 cloves garlic, chopped

3 tbsp. fresh ginger, chopped

3 tbsp. olive oil

15 oz. can garbanzo beans, rinsed and drained

1 cup tomato juice

¼ cup potato flakes

½ cup plain Greek yogurt

Fresh cilantro, chopped for garnish

Directions

1.   Combine all dry spices and toss with lamb in a mixing bowl.

2.   Add onions, garlic and ginger to bowl. Cover and refrigerate 1-4 hours.

3.   Place the inner pot in cooker. Push CHICKEN/MEAT button and the time adjustment button to reach 30 minutes (or high pressure 30 min).

4.   When inner pot is preheated, add olive oil and sear lamb.

5.   Add garbanzos, tomato juice and place lid on pressure cooker. Lock the lid and switch the pressure valve to CLOSED.

6.   When timer reaches 0, switch the pressure valve to OPEN. Once the steam is released, remove the lid.

7.   Stir in potato flakes to thicken. Stir, then add yogurt. Garnish with cilantro.

Eric's Tip: Serve with naan bread for a delicious wrap!

Seafood

If you only used your pressure cooker for seafood, it would be worth the price of admission. The first time I used mine, I made clams with rice. I was really skeptical pressure would be a benefit to something from the sea. I soon found out that pressure cooking does indeed make cooking seafood fast, easy and delicious. The flavor of the seafood is infused into what ever you might be cooking it with and the spices you use get infused into the broth that is left over. It's a win-win! Most seafood like mussels, clams, lobsters, etc. will only take a few minutes, and what's great is you don't have to monitor the pot if you are using the Power Pressure Cooker XL or another electric pressure cooker with an auto shut off. This takes the pressure off of you.

Cooking delicate cuts of fish work amazingly well. Since you do not have to flip the fish, it cooks in one pot in a very short time. I always cook my delicate fish on a steamer rack which also will make it easy to lift the fish out of the pressure cooker. With all seafood, be sure to serve it immediately. This is one food group that doesn't benefit from sitting around. Remember the sauce or broth that is left over will be full of flavor. Save it and serve it over pasta if there is any leftover.

Fresh Clams with Chorizo and Rice

Ingredients

3 tbsp. olive oil

2 cups Arborio Rice

8 oz. cured spicy chorizo, medium diced

2 (16 oz.) cans Italian style white clam sauce

1 cup white wine (preferably sauvignon blanc)

Zest and juice of one lemon

50 littleneck clams

½ cup Parmesan cheese

½ cup chopped basil

Salt and pepper to taste

Directions

1. Place the inner pot in the pressure cooker. Place the oil in the inner pot. Press the RICE/RISOTTO button. Press the time adjustment to reach 8 min. (or 8 min. high pressure).

2. Add olive oil. When the oil is hot, sauté the chorizo for 2 minutes.

3. Add rice and sauté for 2 more minutes, stirring frequently.

4. Add the wine, white clam sauce and lemon juice. Stir.

5. Add the clams on top.

6. Place the lid on the pressure cooker, lock the lid and switch the pressure release valve to CLOSED.

7. Once the timer reaches 0, switch the pressure release valve to OPEN. When the steam is completely released, remove the lid.

8. Scoop out the clams that remained on top (don't worry if some rice gets mixed in) and place them in a serving bowl.

9. Plate the risotto and top with the additional clams. Sprinkle with Parmesan, fresh basil and lemon zest. Salt and pepper to taste.

Eric's Tip: This works well as an appetizer or as a dinner. Add some extra beef stock before reheating leftovers.

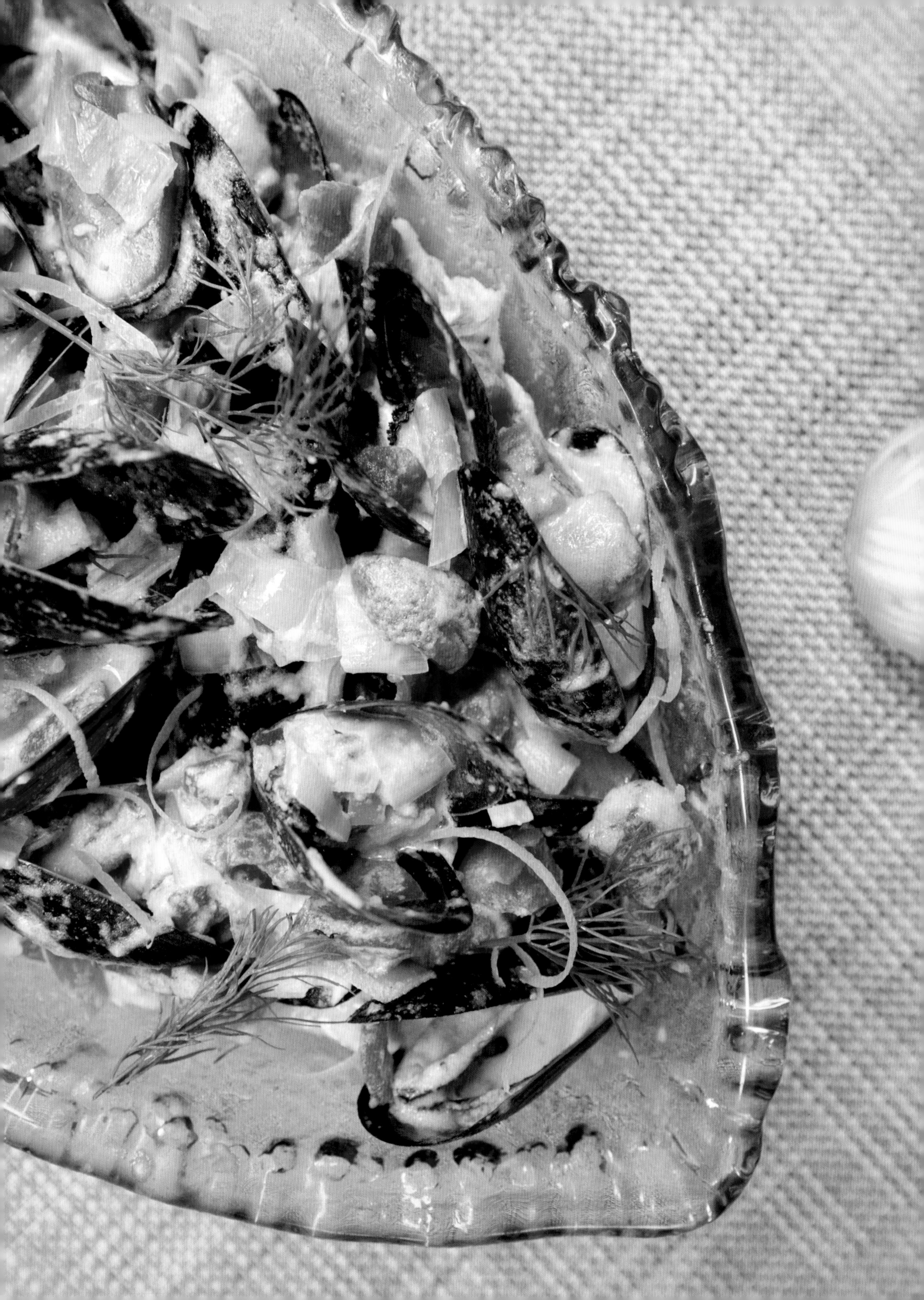

Mussels Dijonaise

Ingredients

3 tbsp. olive oil

1 clove garlic, crushed

2 cups leeks, ½-inch sliced and cleaned

4 lbs. mussels, cleaned and beards removed

1 cup white wine

3 tbsp. Dijon mustard

1¼ cups of cream

2 (14.5 oz.) cans diced tomatoes, drained

¼ cup instant potato flakes for thickening (optional)

1 tsp. lemon zest

2 tbsp. fresh dill, chopped

Salt and pepper

Directions

1.   Place inner pot in the pressure cooker. Press the FISH/VEG/STEAM button and hit the time adjustment button until it reaches 4 min. (or 4 min. high pressure).

2.   Add olive oil, leeks and garlic, and sweat for 5 minutes.

3.   Add mussels, wine, Dijon, salt and pepper.

4.   Place the lid on the pressure cooker, lock the lid, and switch the pressure valve to CLOSED.

5.   Once the timer reaches 0, switch the pressure valve to OPEN. When the steam is completely released, remove the lid.

6.   Remove the mussels using a large spoon to a large serving bowl and cover to keep warm. Discard any unopened mussels.

7.   Add cream to the sauce in the inner pot and press the SOUP/STEW button. Simmer for about 7 minutes. If further thickening is desired, sprinkle in instant potato flakes until desired consistency is reached. Add diced tomatoes and stir.

8.   Pour the sauce over the mussels and garnish with fresh dill and lemon rind.

Eric's Tip: Sometimes I like to pull the mussels out of the shells and use them to make delicious pasta sauce.

Ingredients

For the Glaze:

3 tbsp. honey

3 tbsp. balsamic vinegar

¾ tsp. chopped garlic

¾ tsp. Dijon mustard

Salmon and Pilaf:

2 tbsp. oil

1 cup diced onions

2 tsp. minced garlic

½ cup sliced sun dried tomatoes

2¼ cups brown rice

3¾ cups vegetable stock

¾ tsp. dried thyme

1 tsp. dried oregano

1 tsp. salt

½ tsp. black pepper

4 (6 oz.) salmon filets, about an inch thick, seasoned with salt and pepper

¼ cup fresh basil, julienned

Balsamic Glazed Salmon with Tomato Brown Rice Pilaf

Directions

1.   In a small bowl make the glaze by combining the honey, balsamic, garlic and mustard.

2.   Place inner pot into cooker, and press the MEAT/CHICKEN button and the time adjustment button to reach 35 min. (35 minutes high pressure).

3.   Add the oil. When the oil is hot, add onions and 2 tsp. garlic. Sauté for 2 minutes.

4.   Add the sun-dried tomatoes, rice, stock, thyme, oregano, salt, pepper and stir together.

5.   Place the steamer rack into the inner pot carefully (will be hot).

6.   Salt and pepper the salmon filets, then place salmon filets on rack.

7.   Place the lid on the cooker, lock the lid, and switch the pressure valve to CLOSED.

8.   When the timer reaches 0, switch the pressure valve to OPEN. When steam is completely released, open lid.

9.   Carefully transfer salmon to a platter, removing the rack.

10. Stir basil into rice, and then serve with glaze.

Eric's Tip: This doesn't always have to be served hot; this makes for a delicious chilled summer salad as well.

5

Minutes Under
Pressure

SERVES 6 – 8

Ingredients

3 tbsp. olive oil

4 lbs. mussels, cleaned

¼ lb. bacon, chopped

3 tbsp. garlic, chopped

2 tbsp. capers

2 shallots, chopped

1 each fennel bulb, chopped

1 cup white wine

1 (28 oz.) can diced tomatoes

2 tsp. red pepper flakes

1 tbsp. Sriracha sauce

¼ cup Italian parsley, chopped

Mussels Fra Diavolo

Directions

1.   Push FISH/VEG/STEAM button and time adjustment button to reach 5 minutes (5 min. high pressure).

2.   With the lid off, heat oil and add bacon. Cook until crispy.

3.   Add garlic, shallots, capers, fennel and pepper flakes and Sriracha. Sauté for 2 minutes.

4.   Deglaze with wine then add mussels.

5.   Pour tomatoes over mussels.

6.   Place lid on cooker, lock the lid, and switch the pressure valve to CLOSED.

7.   When the timer reaches 0, switch the pressure valve to OPEN. Once all the pressure is released, open the lid.

8.   Pour mussels and sauce into a big serving bowl and garnish with parsley.

5
Minutes Under
Pressure

SERVES 6 – 8

Ingredients

3 tbsp. olive oil

4 lbs. mussels, cleaned

½ lb. kielbasa, chopped

2 cups white onion, julienned

1 clove garlic, chopped

12 oz. quality lager

2 tbsp. whole-grain mustard

1 tsp. caraway seed

1 cup chicken broth

½ cup heavy cream

½ cup Gorgonzola crumbles

¼ cup Italian parsley, chopped

Olde Country Mussels

Directions

1.   Add oil to the inner pot.

2.   Push FISH/VEG/STEAM button then the time adjustment button to reach 5 min. (or 5 min. high pressure).

3.   Once the oil is hot, brown the kielbasa and onions for 5-6 minutes.

4.   Add garlic, caraway seed and mustard, and then stir.

5.   Add lager, chicken broth and mussels.

6.   Place lid on pressure cooker. Lock the lid and switch the pressure valve to CLOSED.

7.   When timer reaches 0, switch the pressure valve to OPEN. Once the steam is released, remove the lid.

8.   Spoon mussels out on to a serving dish.

9.   Add heavy cream and parsley to the sauce in pot, then stir and heat for 3 minutes.

10. Sprinkle Gorgonzola over mussels, and then pour sauce on top.

5

Minutes Under
Pressure

SERVES 8 – 10

Ingredients

½ lb. bacon, diced

1 tsp. garlic, minced

1 cup onions, diced

2½ cups 5-minute,
quick cooking grits

7 cups water or vegetable stock

2 tbsp. butter

3 tsp. salt

½ tsp. black pepper

2 lbs. large frozen shrimp,
peeled, deveined and tail off

4 cups cheddar cheese, grated

1 cup scallions, sliced

Cheesy Grits and Shrimp with Scallions

Directions

1. Place inner pot in cooker.

2. Hit the BEANS/LENTILS button (or 5 minutes high pressure).

3. Once the pot is preheated, add the bacon and sauté until crispy (you may need to drain the fat halfway through to achieve crispiness).

4. Add the garlic and onions and sweat for another 2 minutes.

5. Add the grits, water or stock, butter, salt, pepper and shrimp.

6. Stir together.

7. Place lid on the cooker, lock the lid and switch the pressure valve to CLOSED.

8. When timer reaches 0, switch the pressure valve to OPEN.

9. When the steam is completely released, open lid.

10. Stir, and then fold in the cheese and scallions until cheese has melted.

11. Serve.

Eric's Tip: I like to garnish this dish with some fresh Pico de Gallo or bruschetta topping.

SERVES 6 – 8

Bouillabaisse

Ingredients

3 tbsp. olive oil

1 lb. mussels, cleaned

1 lb. shrimp,
peeled and deveined

1 lb. clams, cleaned

1 lb. firm fish such as mahi mahi
or snapper, cut into 2-inch pieces

1 cup clam juice

½ cup white wine

1 (28 oz.) can of diced tomatoes

1 large onion, sliced

1 fennel bulb, sliced

1 tsp. ground coriander

1 tbsp. Sriracha

4 cloves garlic, chopped

Pinch of saffron

2 each orange peel, 1" x 2"

Salt and pepper to taste

Directions

1.   Push FISH/VEG/STEAM button and time adjustment button
to reach 4 minutes (or 4 min. high pressure).

2.   Add oil to the inner pot.

3.   Once the oil is hot, add onions, fennel, coriander, garlic and
orange peel. Sauté for 3 minutes.

4.   Deglaze with wine, then add clam juice, tomatoes, saffron and
Sriracha. Stir well.

5.   Add mussels, clams, shrimp and fish. Lock lid into place and
switch the pressure valve to CLOSED.

6.   When timer reaches 0, switch pressure valve to OPEN and,
once the pressure has been released, remove lid.

7.   Serve.

Eric's Tip: Add your fresh herbs at the end to keep the
flavors bright.

Saucy Asian Shrimp

Ingredients

4 lbs. frozen shrimp,
uncooked and peeled

1 cup clam juice (or fish stock)

1 cup white wine

2 bay leaves

1 tbsp. dried cilantro

Juice of 1 lemon

For the sauce:

1 cup mayonnaise

3 tbsp. Thai chili sauce (Sriracha)

3 tbsp. toasted sesame oil

2 cloves garlic, smashed

1 Thai chili pepper, sliced

4 tbsp. soy sauce

1 fresh lime, zest and juice

1 tbsp. brown sugar

1 tbsp. fresh ginger julienned

For the garnish:

¼ cup fresh cilantro leaves

¼ cup fresh basil leaves

1 scallion, 1-inch sliced

2 tbsp. toasted sesame seed

Directions

1.   Place inner pot in the pressure cooker. Place shrimp, clam juice, wine, bay leaves, dried cilantro, lemon juice in the inner pot. Stir.

2.   Place the lid on the pressure cooker, lock the lid and switch the pressure valve to CLOSED.

3.   Press the FISH/VEG/STEAM button and then press the time adjustment button until you reach 7 min. (or 7 min. high pressure).

4.   While the shrimp is cooking, in a separate bowl make the sauce. Combine the sauce ingredients and whisk until well combined.

5.   Once the timer reaches 0, switch the pressure release valve to OPEN. When the steam is completely released, remove the lid and remove and strain shrimp.

6.   Dispose of the remaining cooking liquid and bay leaves, and replace inner pot.

7.   Add the shrimp back into the pot, pour the sauce overtop and stir to coat the shrimp. When the shrimp is coated well and heated through, top with garnish and serve.

Eric's Tip: Enjoy as a simple appetizer, or serve over rice for a heartier dish.

Ingredients

1 tsp. salt

1 tsp. black pepper

1 tsp. paprika

1 tsp. cumin

1 tsp. cayenne pepper

¼ tsp. ground nutmeg

¼ tsp. ground cardamom

2 lbs. fresh boneless, skinless fish fillets (ex: snapper, mahi mahi, etc)

½ lb. shrimp, peeled and deveined

½ lb. scallops

2 tbsp. olive oil

1 can unsweetened coconut milk

2 tbsp. red curry paste

1 green bell pepper, sliced

1 red bell pepper, sliced

1 yellow bell pepper, sliced

1 medium red onion, sliced

3 cloves garlic, chopped

3 tbsp. fresh ginger, chopped

1/3 cup fresh cilantro, chopped

¼ cup fresh basil, chiffonade

1 fresh jalapeño, seeded and chopped

1 fresh lime, cut into wedges

"Toss and Go" Island Fish Stew

Directions

1. Combine salt, pepper, paprika, cayenne, nutmeg, and cardamom. Season the fish, shrimp and scallops with this spice rub.

2. Push FISH/VEG/STEAM button, and push time adjustment button to reach 6 min. (6 min. high pressure).

3. In a separate bowl, mix the coconut milk, curry paste, and ginger.

4. Pour the coconut mixture into the inner pot. Add the peppers and onions and stir.

5. Layer shrimp, scallops and fish on top of vegetables.

6. Lock the lid into place and switch the pressure valve to CLOSED.

7. When timer reaches 0, switch the pressure valve to OPEN. Once the steam is released, remove the lid.

8. Gently remove the fish, shrimp and scallops and plate them.

9. Stir in cilantro, basil and jalapeno, then pour liquid over the seafood.

10. Garnish with fresh squeezed lime wedges.

Eric's Tip: If you can't find fresh fish to your liking, you can use quality IQF fish that is thawed to the package directions.

6
Minutes Under Pressure

SERVES 4 – 6

Ingredients

1 (15 oz.) can white clam sauce

1 cup dry white wine

1 tsp. Old Bay seasoning

6 cloves garlic

1 tbsp. seafood boil seasoning

1 tbsp. black pepper

1 tsp. crushed red pepper
(optional)

12 small red potatoes, quartered

1 lb. kielbasa,
cut into 2-inch slices

1 lb. andouille sausage,
cut into 2-inch slices

5 ears of corn,
shucked and cut into thirds

3 lbs. shrimp, shells on

2 lbs. mussels, cleaned

3 fresh lemons, halved

2 sticks butter

½ cup fresh cilantro, chopped

"Toss and Go" Lil' Jesse's Low Country Boil

Directions

1.   Press the RICE/RISOTTO button on the pressure cooker (6 minutes high pressure).

2.   Add all ingredients.

3.   Place the lid on the cooker, lock the lid and switch the pressure valve to CLOSED.

4.   When the timer reaches zero, switch the pressure valve to OPEN, release the pressure and then remove the lid.

5.   Line a large sheet pan with newspaper and dump contents carefully (will be hot). Drizzle butter over the top and sprinkle fresh cilantro.

Eric's Tip: **For vegetarian option, use the following substitutes:**

- **Substitute clam sauce with vegetable broth.**
- **Substitute kielbasa, sausage, shrimp and mussels with eggplant, kale and carrots.**

Vegetarian

Often I hear folks tell me that they are vegetarian and don't think a pressure cooker can be an asset to them. That couldn't be more false. Cooking veggies and grains in a pressure cooker is not only fast and efficient but also it captures the nutrients in the pot so none of the good stuff goes down the drain, not to mention that you are infusing your food with flavor. This goes for veggies, beans, rice and any grain!

Most veggies only take a few minutes to cook under pressure. Like any technique, you will get more adept as you use the pressure cooker. Using time charts are fine, but I feel that everyone has a different idea of when done is "done." Some folks like their veggies cooked soft while others like them al dente. I say eat them the way you like them! You can use these recipes as a general rule for cooking just about anything. I encourage you to get creative and make some great veggies or vegan meals in minutes that are full of flavor!

Ingredients

1 cup black beans

2 tbsp. oil

1 medium onion, sliced

2 red pepper, julienned

1 green pepper, julienned

1 (14.5 oz.) can petite diced tomatoes

1 (1.12 oz.) package fajita seasoning

1½ cups long-grain rice

1¼ cups vegetable stock

¼ cup fresh cilantro, chopped

10-12 flour tortillas

Fixings: salsa, guacamole, lime wedges

Rice and Black Bean Fajitas

Directions

1. Place inner pot in cooker.

2. Add beans and cover with an inch of water.

3. Place the lid on the cooker and switch the pressure valve to CLOSED.

4. Press the BEANS/LENTILS button once (or high pressure for 10 min).

5. Lock the lid and switch the pressure valve to CLOSED.

6. When the timer reaches 0, hit the warm/cancel button (or off/cxl).

7. Let the pressure in the cooker release naturally without opening pressure valve.

8. When pressure has dropped, remove lid.

9. Drain beans and set aside.

10. Place inner pot in cooker.

11. Add oil, onions and peppers.

12. Press the BEANS/LENTILS button (or 10 min. high pressure).

13. Once the oil is hot, sauté onions and peppers for about 5 minutes without lid.

14. Add the tomatoes, fajita seasoning, rice, vegetable stock and beans.

15. Place the lid on the cooker and switch the pressure valve to CLOSED.

16. When the timer reaches 0, switch the pressure valve to OPEN.

17. When the steam is completely released, open lid.

18. Stir in cilantro.

19. Serve with tortillas and fixings.

Lentil Moussaka

Ingredients

2 tbsp. olive oil

1 cup onion, diced

2 tsp. garlic, chopped

5 cups eggplant, diced

1 (14.5 oz.) can petite diced tomatoes

1 tbsp. tomato paste

1 tsp. dried oregano

1 tsp. ground cumin

½ tsp. ground cinnamon

2 tsp. salt

½ tsp. ground black pepper

1½ cups dried lentils

2 cups vegetable broth

2 cups Greek yogurt

1 cup feta cheese, crumbled

Directions

1. Place the inner pot into the cooker.

2. Press the SOUP/STEW button once (high pressure 10 minutes).

3. Add the oil, and when the oil is hot, sauté the onion and garlic for 2 minutes.

4. Add eggplant and sauté for another 2 minutes.

5. Add the diced tomatoes, tomato paste, oregano, cumin, cinnamon, salt, pepper, lentils and vegetable broth and stir together.

6. Place the lid on the pressure cooker, lock the lid and switch the pressure release valve to CLOSED.

7. In a small bowl combine the yogurt and feta. Set aside.

8. Once the cooker reaches 0, switch the pressure release valve to OPEN.

9. When the steam is completely released, open the lid.

10. Serve with a dollop of yogurt and feta mixture.

Eric's Tip: Top the moussaka with a poached egg for a fantastic brunch!

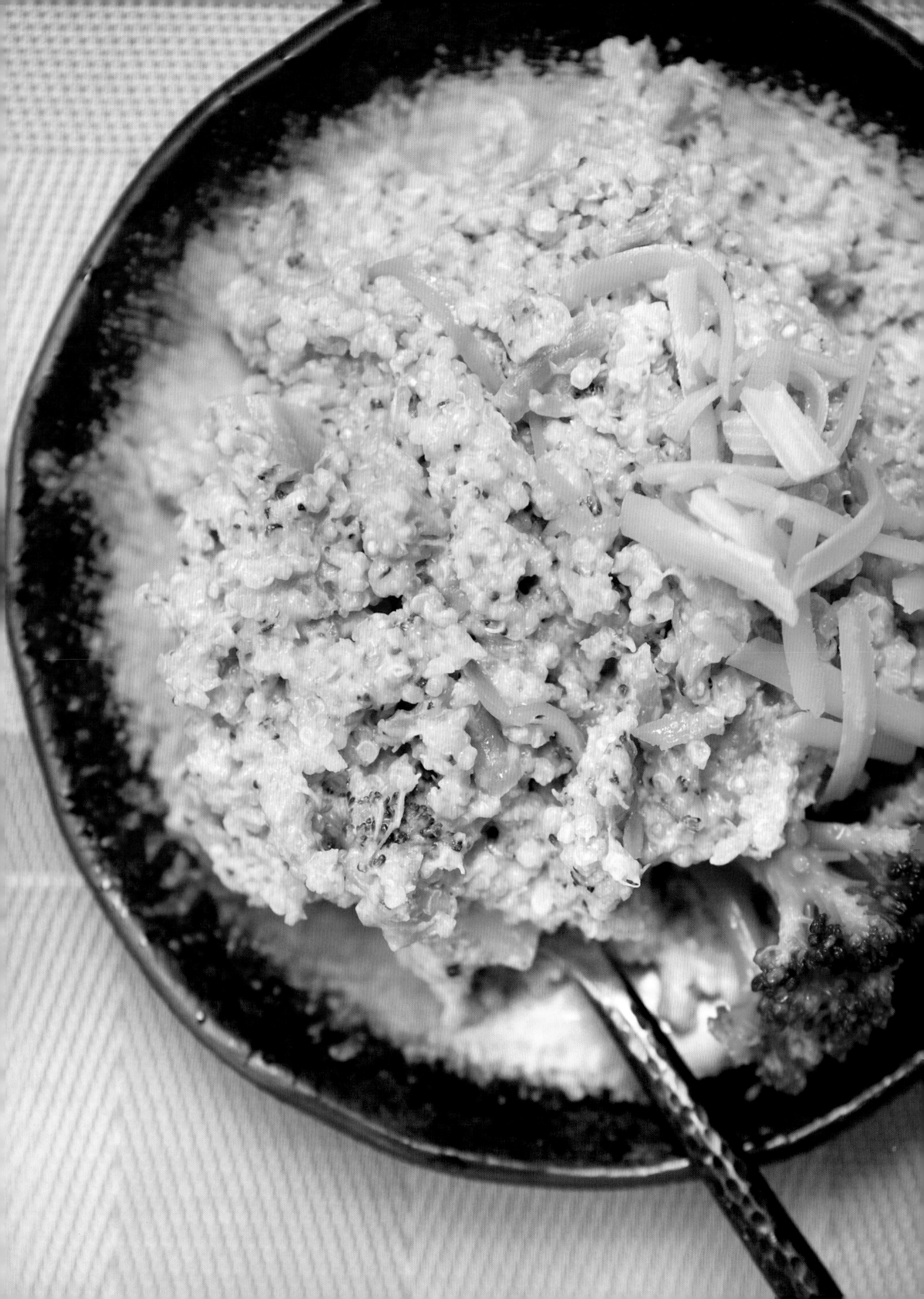

SERVES 6 – 8

Ingredients

2½ cups quinoa

3 cups water

1 (16 oz.) bag of frozen broccoli
florets

1 (14.5 oz.) can evaporated milk

2 tsp. salt

½ tsp. black pepper

½ tsp. mustard powder

4 cups shredded sharp yellow
cheddar

½ cup grated Romano cheese

1 tbsp. butter

4 oz. cream cheese,
room temperature and cut
in ½-inch pieces

Cheesy Broccoli and Quinoa

Directions

1.   Place inner pot in cooker.

2.   Add quinoa, water and broccoli.

3.   Place the lid on the cooker, lock the lid and switch the pressure valve to CLOSED.

4.   Press the FISH/VEG/STEAM button and then hit the time adjustment button until you reach 4 minutes (4 min. high pressure).

5.   While quinoa is cooking, make the milk mixture.

6.   In a bowl combine the evaporated milk, salt, pepper and mustard powder.

7.   When the timer reaches 0, switch the pressure valve to OPEN.

8.   When steam is completely released, open the lid.

9.   Add milk mixture, cheddar, Romano, butter, cream cheese.

10. Stir together.

11. Press the CHICKEN/MEAT button (or brown/sauté mode) and stir until the cheese has melted.

12. Serve.

Eric's Tip: Substitute cauliflower or brussel sprouts for a delicious twist on this recipe!

11

Minutes Under
Pressure

SERVES 8 – 10

Ingredients

2 tsp. garlic, chopped

1 cup onions, medium diced

4 cups butternut squash, large diced

1½ cups pearled barley

3 cups vegetable or chicken stock

3 tsp. salt

½ tsp. pepper

2 tbsp. chopped fresh sage

1 cup Parmesan

2 tbsp. half and half

1 cup toasted walnuts

Butternut Squash Barley with Sage and Toasted Walnuts

Directions

1. Place inner pot in cooker.

2. Add barley and cover with an inch of water.

3. Press the BEANS/LENTILS button (or high pressure 5 min).

4. Place the lid on the cooker, lock the lid and switch the pressure valve to CLOSED.

5. When the timer reaches 0, hit the cancel/warm button (or off/cxl).

6. Let the pressure in the cooker release naturally without opening the pressure valve.

7. Drain barley and set aside.

8. Place inner pot in cooker.

9. Press the RICE/RISOTTO button.

10. Add oil, and when the oil is hot, sauté the garlic and onions for 2 minutes.

11. Add squash, barley, stock, salt, pepper and sage.

12. Place the lid on the cooker, lock the lid and switch the pressure valve to CLOSED.

13. Press RICE/RISOTTO button (6 min. high pressure).

14. When the timer reaches 0, switch the pressure valve to OPEN.

15. When steam is completely released, open the lid.

16. Stir in Parmesan, half and half and walnuts.

17. Serve.

Spanish Quinoa Stuffed Peppers

Ingredients

1 cup dried pinto beans

2 tsp. minced garlic

1 cup diced onions

6 red peppers

1 (14.5 oz.) can petite-diced tomatoes

1 cup quinoa

1 cups vegetable stock

1 tsp. ground cumin

2 tsp. chili powder

2 tsp. salt

½ tsp. black pepper

2 tbsp. chopped cilantro

2 cups shredded cheddar cheese

1 (15 oz.) can tomato sauce

2 (10 oz.) cans of diced tomatoes with chilies

Directions

1.   Place inner pot in cooker. Add the beans and cover with 1 inch of water.
2.   Place the lid on the cooker and switch the pressure valve to CLOSED.
3.   Press the BEANS/LENTILS button then hit the time adjustment button until you reach 7 minutes (or 7 min. high pressure).
4.   When timer reaches zero, hit the cancel/warm button (or off/cxl button).
5.   Let the pressure in the cooker release naturally without opening pressure valve.
6.   When pressure has dropped, remove lid.
7.   Drain beans and set aside.
8.   Slice off the tops of each pepper, remove stem and chop the tops and reserve bottoms.
9.   Place the inner pot in cooker.
10. Press the RICE/RISOTTO button and time adjustment button to reach 8 minutes (8 minutes high pressure).
11. Add oil, and when the oil is hot, add the garlic, onions, chopped pepper tops. Sauté for 3 minutes.
12. Add the tomatoes, quinoa, stock, cumin, chili powder, salt, pepper and beans.
13. Place the lid on the cooker, lock the lid and switch the pressure valve to CLOSED.
14. When the timer reaches 0, switch the pressure valve to OPEN.
15. When steam is completely released, open lid.
16. Spread quinoa and beans on a baking sheet and let cool slightly.
17. Place the inner pot in cooker.
18. Add the tomato sauce and diced tomatoes with chilies.
19. Place the canning rack in the cooker.
20. Hollow the bottoms of the peppers.
21. Place quinoa and beans into a bowl.
22. Stir in the chopped cilantro and 1 cup of cheese into the rice & bean mixture.
23. Fill each pepper with quinoa bean mixture and place on the canning rack.
24. Top each pepper with the remaining cheese.
25. Place the lid on the cooker and switch the pressure valve to CLOSED.
26. Press the FISH/VEG/STEAM button and then hit the time adjust button until you reach 6 minutes (or high pressure 6 minutes).
27. When the timer reaches zero, switch the pressure valve to OPEN.
28. When steam is completely released, open lid.
29. Serve with tomato sauce.

SERVES 10-12

Greek Brown Rice Salad

Ingredients

2 cups brown rice

2 tsp. salt

1 tsp. dried oregano

1 tsp. lemon zest

3 tsp. minced garlic, divided

½ cup red onion, small diced

1½ cups tomato, small diced

1½ cups English cucumber, small diced

¾ cup kalamata olives, halved & pitted

½ cup lemon juice

½ cup olive oil

½ tsp. black pepper

¼ cup fresh parsley, chopped

1½ cups crumbled feta cheese

Directions

1. Place inner pot in cooker.

2. Add rice, 4 cups water, salt, oregano, lemon zest and 1 tsp. garlic.

3. Place the lid on the cooker, lock the lid, and switch the pressure valve to CLOSED.

4. Press the SOUP/STEW button and then hit the time adjustment button until you reach 15 minutes (or 15 min. high pressure).

5. When the timer reaches 0, switch the pressure valve to OPEN.

6. When steam is completely released, open lid.

7. Drain rice and spread on a baking sheet to cool.

8. When rice has cooled, place in a large bowl.

9. Add red onion, tomato, English cucumber, olives, lemon juice, oil, pepper, parsley and remaining garlic.

10. Stir together and then fold in feta cheese.

11. Cover and refrigerate for 1-2 hours. Serve.

Basmati Rice with Sweet Potatoes, Coconut and Curry

Ingredients

2 tbsp. oil

2 tsp. minced garlic

1 cup onions, medium diced

1 cup sweet potatoes, peeled and large diced

2 cups basmati rice

1 (14.5 oz.) can petite diced tomatoes

1 (13.5 oz.) can coconut milk

1 cup vegetable stock

1 tbsp. curry powder

1 tbsp. ginger, minced

1 tbsp. brown sugar

2 tsp. salt

½ tsp. pepper

¼ cup fresh cilantro, chopped

Directions

1.   Place inner pot in cooker.

2.   Press the RICE/RISOTTO button (or high pressure 6 min).

3.   Add the garlic and onions and sauté for 2 minutes.

4.   Add sweet potatoes, rice, tomatoes, coconut milk, stock, curry powder, ginger, brown sugar, salt and pepper. Stir.

5.   Place the lid on the cooker, lock the lid and switch the pressure valve to CLOSED.

6.   When the timer reaches zero, switch the pressure valve to OPEN.

7.   When steam is completely released, open lid.

8.   Fold in cilantro.

9.   Serve.

Eric's Tip: This makes a fantastic stuffing for vegetarian burritos.

Ingredients

3 tsp. garlic, minced

2 cups onions, large diced

2 cups red peppers, large diced

2 cups carrots, large diced

2 cups mushrooms, sliced

3 cups eggplant, peeled and
large diced

2 cups zucchini, large diced

1 (14.5 oz.) can diced tomatoes

1 (15 oz.) can tomato sauce

½ cup vegetable stock

1 tsp. dried oregano

1 tsp. dried basil

2 tsp. salt

½ tsp. pepper

Dumplings:

½ cup instant couscous

½ cup grated parmesan cheese

2/3 cup all purpose flour

2 tsp. baking powder

½ tsp. salt

2 eggs

2 tsp. olive oil

1/3 cup vegetable stock

¼ cup fresh parsley, chopped

Ratatouille with Parmesan Couscous Dumplings

Directions

1. Place inner pot in cooker.

2. Press the FISH/VEG/STEAM button (or 2 min. high pressure).

3. Add the garlic, onions, peppers, carrots and mushrooms and sauté for about 5 minutes.

4. Add the eggplant, zucchini, diced tomatoes, tomato sauce, vegetable stock, oregano, basil salt and pepper.

5. Stir together.

6. In a bowl combine the couscous, cheese, flour, baking powder and salt.

7. In another bowl combine the eggs, olive oil and stock.

8. Add the wet ingredients to the dry ingredients and stir together until ingredients are combined.

9. Fold in parsley.

10. Place generous tablespoonful's of couscous mixture over surface of ratatouille ingredients.

11. Place the lid on the cooker, lock the lid and switch the pressure valve to CLOSED.

12. When the timer reaches zero, switch the pressure valve to OPEN.

13. When steam is completely released open lid.

14. Serve.

5

Minutes Under
Pressure

SERVES 8 – 10

Lentil Salad with Dried Cherries and Walnuts

Ingredients

2 cups dried lentils

1 bay leaf

2½ cups water

1 cup red onion, small diced

1 cup celery, small diced

¾ cup dried cherries, roughly chopped

1 cup walnuts, chopped and toasted

Juice of 1 lemon

Juice and zest of 2 oranges

2 tbsp. red wine vinegar

¼ cup olive oil

¼ cup fresh parsley, chopped

2 tsp. salt

½ tsp. pepper

Directions

1. Place the inner pot into the cooker.

2. Add the lentils, bay leaf and water.

3. Place the lid on the cooker, lock the lid and switch the pressure valve to CLOSED.

4. Press the BEANS/LENTILS button once (or 5 min. high pressure).

5. When the timer reaches zero, switch the pressure valve to OPEN.

6. When the steam is completely released, open the lid.

7. Drain the lentils and set them aside to cool.

8. When lentils have cooled, place them in large bowl.

9. Add the onion, celery, cherries, walnuts, lemon juice, orange juice and zest, red wine vinegar, olive oil, chopped parsley, salt and pepper.

10. Fold ingredients together.

11. Cover and refrigerate for 1-2 hours before serving.

Wild Rice Salad with Apricots and Almonds

Ingredients

2 cups wild rice

3 tsp. salt, divided

3 cups water

1 cup red onions, small diced

1 cup celery, small diced

¾ cup dried apricots, small diced

1 cup red grapes, halved

1 cup slivered almonds, toasted

1½ cups mayonnaise

2 tbsp. white vinegar

½ tsp. pepper

Directions

1. Put inner pot in cooker.

2. Add rice, 2 tsp. salt and 3 cups water.

3. Place the lid on the cooker and switch the pressure valve to CLOSED.

4. Press the RICE/RISOTTO button, then hit the time adjustment button until you reach 35 minutes (or 35 min. high pressure).

5. When the timer reaches 0, switch the pressure valve to OPEN.

6. When the steam is completely released, open lid.

7. Drain rice and set aside to cool.

8. When rice is cooled, place in a large mixing bowl.

9. Add the red onions, celery, apricots, grapes and almonds.

10. In a small bowl mix together the mayonnaise, vinegar, remaining salt and pepper.

11. Fold into rice mixture.

12. Cover and refrigerate for 1-2 hours before serving.

Ingredients

1½ cup black eyed peas

2 tbsp. oil

3 tsp. minced garlic

1 cup onion, diced

1 green pepper, diced

2 stalks celery, diced

1 (14.5 oz.) can petite diced tomatoes

1 cup long grain white rice

1½ cups diced ham

4 cups chicken stock

Pinch cayenne pepper

1 tsp. dried thyme

2 tsp. salt

¼ cup fresh parsley, chopped

½ tsp. black pepper

Barley Hoppin' John

Directions

1. Place inner pot in cooker.

2. Add peas and cover with an inch of water.

3. Place lid on the cooker, lock the lid and switch the pressure valve to CLOSED.

4. Press the FISH/VEG/STEAM button once (or 2 min high pressure).

5. When the timer reaches zero, switch the pressure valve to OPEN.

6. When steam is completely released, remove lid.

7. Drain peas and set aside.

8. Place inner pot in cooker.

9. Press the SOUP/STEW button (or 10 min. high pressure)

10. Add oil, garlic, pepper and celery and sauté for about 2 minutes.

11. Add the peas, tomatoes, rice, ham, stock, cayenne, thyme, salt and pepper. Stir.

12. Place the lid on the cooker, lock the lid and switch the pressure valve to CLOSED.

13. When the timer reaches 0, switch the pressure valve to OPEN.

14. When steam is completely released, open lid.

15. Stir in fresh parsley.

70
Minutes Under
Pressure

SERVES 6

Individual Wild Rice, Mushroom and Swiss Cheese Quiches

Ingredients

½ cup uncooked wild rice

3 cups water

2 tbsp. oil

1 cup onions, medium diced

8 oz. mushrooms, chopped

½ tsp. dried thyme

1 tsp. salt

¼ tsp. pepper

1½ cups Swiss cheese, grated

1 cup baking mix

1¾ cups milk

4 eggs

Directions

1. Place inner pot in cooker. Add the rice and 1 cup of water.

2. Place the lid on the cooker, lock the lid and switch pressure valve to CLOSED.

3. Press the RICE/RISOTTO button, then hit the time adjustment until you reach 35 minutes (or high pressure 35 min).

4. When the timer reaches 0, switch the pressure valve to OPEN. When steam is completely released, open lid.

5. Drain the rice and place into a bowl. Set aside.

6. Place inner pot in cooker.

7. Press the SOUP/STEW button and time adjustment button to reach 35 minutes (or 35 min. high pressure).

8. Add oil and onion and sauté for 2 minutes. Add mushrooms, thyme, salt and pepper. Cook until moisture from the mushrooms has evaporated.

9. Add the mushrooms and onions to the rice and stir together.

10. Divide the mushroom mixture between six 8–oz. ramekins.

11. Divide Swiss cheese evenly between the ramekins.

12. In a separate bowl combine the baking mix, milk and eggs.

13. Divide the mixture evenly over the cheese in the ramekins.

14. Wrap each ramekin tightly in foil.

15. Place the inner pot in cooker, then place steaming rack in bottom of inner pot.

16. Add 2 cups of water to the inner pot.

17. Place ramekins onto steaming rack, offset stacking them if needed.

18. Place the lid on the cooker, lock the lid and switch the pressure valve to CLOSED.

19. When the timer reaches 0, hit the cancel/warm button (or off/cancel button).

20. Let the steam release without opening the pressure valve.

21. When steam has completely released, open lid.

22. Remove hot ramekins carefully and unwrap.

23. Serve.

Sweets

When I first began using a pressure cooker many years ago, I would never have thought to make breads or desserts in it! Once you get the hang of it, you will want to test your skills and expand your repertoire in the pressure cooker all of the time. In fact, you will even find that egg-based custard types of desserts are much better in the pressure cooker due to the consistent heat and moisture under pressure where this isn't true of the harsh, dry environment inside of your oven.

There are some really fun and delicious recipes in this section. You have to try the corn breads, but after you become comfortable with the basic recipe, be creative and add your own favorite flavors. The same goes for rice puddings. I give you a good base, but then feel free to change it up and make it your own once you're comfortable.

Coconut Joy with Almond Rice Pudding

Ingredients

3 cups Arborio Rice

7 cups whole milk

1 pinch salt

1 cup sugar

½ cup unsweetened coconut milk

1½ cups unsweetened coconut flakes, lightly toasted

1 cup roughly chopped roasted almonds

4 oz. dark chocolate, finely chopped

For garnish: Additional ½ cup coconut flakes and some whole almonds

Directions

1.   Place the inner pot in the pressure cooker. Pour in the rice, milk , sugar, salt, and coconut milk. Stir and press the RICE/RISOTTO button. Press the time adjustment to reach 11 min.

2.   Place the lid on the pressure cooker, lock the lid and switch the pressure release valve to CLOSED.

3.   Once the timer reaches 0, the cooker will automatically switch to keep warm. Switch the pressure release valve to OPEN. When the steam is completely released, remove the lid.

4.   Stir well. Put the lid back on and let sit for 10 minutes. Remove the lid and fold in the coconut, almonds and chocolate.

5.   Check the consistency and add extra milk if too firm, a ¼ cup at a time.

6.   Garnish and serve immediately.

Eric's Tip: Rice pudding is great served warm or cold. If you want to reheat it in the microwave, heat it to desired temperature and then add some milk to reach desired consistency.

Tres Leche Rice Pudding

Ingredients

4 cups Arborio rice

3 cups milk

2 (14 oz.) cans evaporated milk

2 (12 oz.) cans sweetened condensed milk

1 tsp. ground cinnamon

1½ tbsp. vanilla extract

Directions

1.   Place inner pot in cooker.

2.   Add all ingredients and stir well.

3.   Place the lid on the cooker and switch the pressure valve to CLOSED.

4.   Hit the RICE/RISOTTO button and then hit the time adjustment button until you reach 8 minutes (or 8 min. high pressure).

5.   When timer reaches zero, hit the cancel/warm button (or off/cxl button).

6.   Keep the pressure valve closed for 10 minutes, then open to release the rest of the steam.

7.   When steam is completely released, open lid.

8.   Stir and serve.

SERVES 4 – 6

Ingredients

1 ⅓ cups yellow corn meal

⅔ cups all-purpose flour

⅔ cups sugar

1 cup dried figs, fine chopped

2 tsp. fresh orange zest, chopped

3 tsp. baking powder

1 tsp. salt

1 tsp. ground cinnamon

¼ tsp. ground nutmeg

3 tbsp. honey

1 cup buttermilk

2 eggs

¼ cup melted butter

¼ cup sour cream

Cinnamon Fig Cornbread

Directions

1.   Push RICE/RISOTTO button and time adjustment button to reach 30 min. (or high pressure 30 min).

2.   Mix dry ingredients and figs together.

3.   In a separate bowl, whisk wet ingredients together then gently stir into the dry ingredients.

4.   Pour into a greased 7 x 3 ½-inch baking pan or 1 ½ quart soufflé dish.

5.   Pour 1 cup of water into bottom of cooker, place steamer tray into cooker. Gently place cornbread pan on top of steamer tray. Lock the lid and switch the pressure valve to CLOSED.

6.   When timer reaches zero, switch the pressure valve to OPEN. Once the steam is released, remove the lid.

Ingredients

1⅓ cups yellow corn meal

⅔ cups all-purpose flour

⅔ cups sugar

3 tsp. baking powder

2 tsp. salt

3 tbsp. honey

1 cup buttermilk

2 eggs

1 cup whole corn kernels

¼ cup melted butter

¼ cup sour cream

The Moistest Cornbread EVER

Directions

1. Push RICE/RISOTTO button and time adjustment button until you reach 20 min. (or high pressure 20 min).

2. Mix dry ingredients and corn kernels together.

3. In a separate bowl, whisk wet ingredients together then gently stir into the dry ingredients.

4. Pour into a greased 8-inch baking pan.

5. Pour 1 cup of water into bottom of cooker, place steamer tray in cooker. Gently place cornbread pan on top of steamer tray. Lock the lid and switch the pressure valve to CLOSED.

6. When timer reaches zero, switch the pressure valve to OPEN. Once the steam is released, remove the lid.

25
Minutes Under Pressure

SERVES 6 – 8

Ingredients

4 eggs

1 cup sugar

1 cup dark brown sugar

1¼ cup cocoa

½ cup all-purpose flour

2 sticks butter, melted

1 tbsp. instant espresso

½ cup macadamia nuts, chopped

½ tsp. salt

½ tsp. vanilla extract

Cocoa Macadamia Truffle Cake

Directions

1.   Push RICE/RISOTTO button then the time adjustment button to reach 25 minutes (or high pressure 25 min).

2.   Sift both sugars together.

3.   Using a stand or hand mixer, whisk eggs and sugar until thick and light in color.

4.   Sift cocoa and flour and add to egg mixture with espresso, salt, macadamia nuts and vanilla. Gently stir together with spatula.

5.   Pour into a greased and floured 8-inch baking pan.

6.   Add 1 cup of water to cooker and place steamer tray inside.

7.   Place pan on steamer tray. Lock the lid and switch the pressure valve to CLOSED.

8.   When timer reaches zero, switch the pressure valve to OPEN. Once the steam is released, remove the lid.

**YEILDS 36
SQUARES**

Ingredients

4 cups semi-sweet chocolate chips

1 (14 oz.) can sweetened, condensed milk

6 tbsp. butter

1 tsp. vanilla

1 cup almonds or peanuts

2 cups mini marshmallows

Rocky Road Fudge

Directions

1.   In a metal bowl that will fit inside the inner pot of the pressure cooker, combine the chocolate chips and the sweetened condensed milk. Stir in the tablespoons of butter. Cover the bowl tightly with aluminum foil.

2.   Place the steaming rack on the bottom of the pressure cooker and add 2 cups of water.

3.   Place bowl on top of the rack.

4.   Place the lid on pressure cooker, lock the lid and switch the pressure valve to CLOSED.

5.   Press the BEANS/LENTILS button once (or 5 minutes high pressure).

6.   When the timer reaches 0, switch pressure release valve to open. When the steam is completely released, open the lid.

7.   Carefully take bowl out of the cooker and remove the aluminum foil. Bowl will be hot! Whisk until chocolate chips are melted and mixture is smooth. Let sit for 5 minutes.

8.   Stir in the nuts. Gently fold in the mini marshmallows just until combined. Pour fudge into a greased 9x9 dish. Let fudge cool completely.

9.   Cut fudge into 36 squares and enjoy.

60 Minutes Under Pressure

SERVES 6 – 8

Ingredients

¼ cup butter

1½ cups flour

¾ cup sugar

½ tsp. baking soda

1/8 tsp. salt

1 tsp. cinnamon

2 eggs

¾ cup vegetable oil

¼ cup sour cream

1 tsp. vanilla extract

2 cups small-diced apples

Crumb Topping:

½ cup butter, melted

¾ cup flour

¾ cup sugar

1 tsp. cinnamon

Glaze:

½ cup powdered sugar

1 tbsp. milk

Apple Crumb Cake

Directions

1.   In a large bowl cream together butter and sugar. Add flour, sugar, baking soda, salt and cinnamon. Add eggs, oil, sour cream and vanilla. Mix well. Fold in diced apples. Pour in a greased 7-inch cake pan.

2.   To make crumb topping, mix together melted butter, flour, sugar and cinnamon with a fork to form coarse crumbles. Sprinkle evenly on top of cake batter. Cover with aluminum foil.

3.   Add 1.5 cups of water to the inner pot. Place a steaming rack inside the inner pot of the pressure cooker and then place cake pan on the rack. Place the lid on pressure cooker, lock the lid and switch the pressure valve to CLOSED.

4.   Press the CHICKEN/MEAT button three times to reach 60 min. (or 60 minutes high pressure).

5.   When the timer reaches 0, switch pressure release valve to OPEN. When the steam is completely released, open the lid.

6.   Carefully remove cake pan (will be hot), uncover and let cool.

7.   To make glaze, whisk together powdered sugar and milk until smooth. Drizzle over cake before serving.

Eric's Tip: Using crisp Bosc pears instead of apples is a delicious alternative.

Peach and Blueberry Cobbler

Ingredients

2 (16 oz.) bags frozen sliced peaches, thawed

2 cups blueberries

¾ cup sugar

1 tsp. cinnamon

½ cup cornstarch

2¼ cups Bisquick baking mix

2/3 cup milk

½ cup sugar

¼ tsp. cinnamon

1 tbsp. sugar

Directions

1.   In a large bowl, mix sliced peaches and blueberries together.

2.   Combine ¾ cup sugar, cornstarch, and 1 tsp. cinnamon together. Add it to the peaches and blueberries. Toss gently to coat the fruit. Pour in a 2 qt. baking dish that will fit in the pressure cooker.

3.   Mix together the Bisquick, milk, and ½ cup sugar, and stir until a soft dough is formed. Spread the mixture on top of the fruit.

4.   Mix the ½ tsp. cinnamon and 1 tbsp. sugar together and sprinkle evenly on top. Coat a sheet of aluminum foil with cooking spray and loosely cover the baking dish forming a tent over it.

5.   Place the dish in the inner pot on a rack and add 1½ cups of water. Press the CHICKEN/MEAT button and then press the time adjustment button until it reaches 55 minutes (or 55 min. high pressure).

6.   When the timer reaches 0, the Power Pressure Cooker will automatically switch to the keep warm setting. Turn the cooker off and let dish rest in the cooker until steam is completely released naturally. Do not switch pressure valve to open. Remove the lid.

7.   Serve cobbler warm with vanilla ice cream.

Rum Raisin French Toast Bread Pudding

Ingredients

4 tbsp. butter, melted

½ cup packed brown sugar

1 (12 oz.) can sweetened condensed milk

1 cup whole milk

3 eggs beaten

1 tsp. vanilla

½ tbsp. rum extract

½ tsp. ground cinnamon

¼ tsp. salt

8 cups cubed day-old or toasted Challah bread

¾ cups golden raisins

1 cup water

¼ cup powdered confectioner's sugar

Directions

1.   In a large bowl, whisk together butter, brown sugar, canned milk, whole milk, beaten eggs, vanilla, rum extract, cinnamon and salt.

2.   Add cubed Challah bread and golden raisins to the mixture and let sit for 20 minutes.

3.   Place bread mixture in to a 2-3 quart ceramic bowl or casserole dish that will fit into the pressure cooker pot.

4.   To the pressure cooker pot, place the steaming rack and 1 cup of water. Place the ceramic bowl onto the rack.

5.   Press the RICE/RISOTTO button and time adjustment button until you reach 20 min. (or high pressure 20 minutes).

6.   Place the lid on the cooker, lock the lid and switch the pressure valve to CLOSED.

7.   When the timer has reached 0, switch the pressure valve to OPEN. Once the pressure has been released, open the lid.

8.   Carefully remove ceramic dish/bowl (will be hot) and sprinkle with powdered sugar.

2
Minutes Under Pressure

YIELDS ABOUT 2 CUPS

Ingredients

12 oz. dark chocolate chunks

7 oz. fresh heavy whipping cream

1 oz. peppermint extract

Peppermint Patty Chocolate Fondue

Directions

1. Place all ingredients into a 2-quart ceramic bowl.

2. To the pressure cooker inner pot, add 1 cup of water and the steaming rack.

3. Place bowl onto the center of the steaming rack of pressure cooker.

4. Lock the lid, switch the pressure valve to CLOSED, and press FISH/VEG/STEAM button (2 min. high pressure).

5. Once the timer has reached 0, switch the pressure valve to OPEN. Once the pressure has been fully released, carefully remove the bowl (will be hot) and stir vigorously until smooth.

18
Minutes Under Pressure

SERVES 4

Ingredients

6 oz. chocolate almond biscotti, divided

2 tbsp. butter, melted

6 oz. Ricotta cheese

8 oz. Mascarpone cheese (room temperature)

1/3 cup sugar

1 tbsp. vanilla

2 eggs, beaten

¼ cup white chocolate liqueur

2 oz. dark chocolate chips

2 oz. white chocolate chips

Chocolate sauce for garnish

Black and White Biscotti Cheesecake

Directions

1.   In a food processor or blender, mix 4 oz. of chocolate almond biscotti and melted butter. Pulse until a fine crumb mixture forms.

2.   Divide the biscotti crust mixture into four 8 oz. ramekins. Press crust mixture to the bottom of each ramekin and chill for 20 minutes.

3.   While the ramekins are chilling, into the pitcher of a blender add Ricotta cheese, Mascarpone cheese, sugar, vanilla, eggs, and liqueur. Pulse blender until mixture is well blended. Stir dark and white chocolate chips into the mixture with a spatula or wooden spoon.

4.   Ladle cheesecake mixture into the 4 chilled ramekins. Cover each ramekin with loosely tented aluminum foil. To the pressure cooker inner pot, add 1½ cups of water and the steaming rack. Place all 4 ramekins onto the steaming rack (offset stack them if necessary). Cook at low pressure for 18 minutes. Use natural release method, remove ramekins and chill for 4 hours.

5.   Garnish with remaining 2 oz. of chopped biscotti and drizzle with chocolate sauce.

Eric's Tip: The easiest way to eat these is right out of the ramekin, but for a more formal presentation, you can release them onto a plate and finish the plate with a dramatic drizzle of chocolate.

231

MAKES 6 CUPS

Apple Sauce

Ingredients

3 lbs. Granny Smith apples, peeled, cored and quartered

3/4 tsp. pumpkin pie spice

1/3 cup apple cider or unsweetened apple juice

1/3 cup water

Cinnamon sticks

Directions

1.   Press the RICE/RISOTTO button on the pressure cooker (or 6 min. high pressure).

2.   Place all ingredients into the pressure cooker.

3.   Place pressure lid on, lock the lid and switch the pressure valve to CLOSED.

4.   When timer reaches 0, switch the pressure release valve to OPEN and, once all the pressure has been removed, remove the lid.

5.   Mash apples and serve with whole cinnamon sticks.

10
Minutes Under Pressure

SERVES 8 – 10

"Toss and Go" Apple Cinnamon Steel-Cut Oatmeal

Ingredients

2 cups steel-cut oats

3 cups water

2 cups milk

2 tsp. ground cinnamon

1 tbsp. vanilla extract

½ cup brown sugar

3 granny smith apples, peeled, seeded and large diced

1 generous pinch of salt

Directions

1. Place inner pot in cooker.

2. Add all ingredients and stir together.

3. Place lid on the cooker and switch the pressure valve to CLOSED.

4. Hit the SOUP/STEW button (or 10 min. high pressure).

5. When timer reaches zero, switch the pressure valve to OPEN.

6. When steam is completely released, open the lid.

7. Stir well and serve.

Eric's Tip: I love to add texture to my oatmeal. Try sprinkling either granola or dried, diced fruits to the top as a delicious garnish.

**YIELDS 10 – 14
Small Tamales**

Pineapple Caramel Tamales

Ingredients

1 package corn husks, soaked in warm water

1 (20 oz.) can crushed pineapple

2 cups instant tamale masa flour

1 tsp. baking powder

½ tsp. ground cinnamon

3 tbsp. sugar

1 tsp. salt

⅔ cup vegetable shortening

¼ cup water

20-28 pieces soft caramel candies

Directions

1.   In a separate bowl, combine tamale masa, baking powder, sugar, cinnamon and salt.

2.   Add pineapple, shortening and water. Knead with hands until everything is combined.

3.   Place ⅓ cup of masa mixture in center of corn husk and lightly pat flat.

4.   Place 2 caramel candies in the center and fold the masa around the caramel.

5.   Loosely fold the side of the husk over the masa, then the bottom of the husk, then roll leaving one end open.

6.   Place canning rack in bottom of the inner pot, then add enough water to cover bottom.

7.   Place tamales in pressure cooker standing up with open end up.

8.   Lock lid into place, press BEANS/LENTILS button and adjust time to 20 minutes (20 min. high pressure).

9.   When timer reaches zero, switch the pressure valve to OPEN. Once the steam is released, remove the lid.

Eric's Tip: Topping these warm tamales with ice cream will put you in an even happier happy place.

Index